The New Vic Theatr

Flamingoland

by Deborah McAndrew

Flamingoland was first performed on
Friday 25 July 2008 at the New Vic Theatre

A New Vic Production

Flamingoland

by Deborah McAndrew

Cast

DAVE	Paul Barnhill
BRIDIE	Tina Gray
SADIE	Becky Hindley
MARI	Tricia Kelly
KATHLEEN	Nicola Sanderson

Creative Team

Director	Gwenda Hughes
Designer	Lis Evans
Lighting Designer	Daniella Beattie
Co-Lighting Designer	Peter Morgan
Sound Designer	James Earls-Davis
Voice Coach	Mark Langley

Set and made props by the New Vic Workshop
Costumes by the New Vic Costume Department

Lighting and sound operated by Daniella Beattie,
James Earls-Davis, Peter Morgan and Chloe Baxter

Foreword

Deborah McAndrew's play was just a ghost when we first met. Script, a new writing development organisation, had sent me an anonymous piece titled *Vacuum* which I was to read and report back on. I was impressed. I wrote a positive report recommending it for further attention, and later had a call from Script. *Vacuum* had received more positive feedback from other readers, and Script wanted to offer the writer some mentoring sessions to work on a new idea. Would I be interested in being the mentor?

I'm always daunted by anything that involves the onerous title 'Mentor'. But I wanted to work with this writer, who turned out to be Deborah, so agreed.

Over three meetings, starting with a sketchy first draft of a first act of a play that would become *Flamingoland*, Deborah and I tugged and pushed and nit-picked at the text. In between she developed and rewrote; I digested successive drafts. Finally we reviewed what we'd done and previewed how the play would develop from there. I also took the opportunity to ask her for some inside gossip on her local theatre (the New Vic) – where I had an interview the following week.

Flamingoland and I parted company for a while. I was busy finding my feet at the New Vic. Meanwhile, Deborah was developing the play and her writing career. As she went from strength to strength I began to think: the New Vic is Deborah's local theatre, and I've had a long and happy relationship with *Flamingoland*. I became more and more convinced that we should be responsible for Deborah's first main stage production. I asked Gwenda Hughes, another Staffordshire resident and my predecessor as New Vic Artistic Director, to direct the play. And I'm delighted to say here it is, that rare treasure: a new play on a main stage.

Theresa Heskins
Artistic Director

New Vic Theatre

The New Vic is the regional producing theatre for Staffordshire. With ten major productions a year, it presents a varied and adventurous programme that includes contemporary drama, new commissions, acclaimed operas, innovative adaptations and accessible classics. There is a vibrant relationship between audience and performer, the result of the auditorium entirely surrounding the stage.

Alongside this professional work, under Artistic Directors Gwenda Hughes and, since 2007, Theresa Heskins, the company has developed an extensive and award-winning community involvement with an Education Department and ground-breaking New Vic *Borderlines* undertaking work of international significance.

> '*The New Vic has always had its windows open to allow air from the community to blow through.*' Mike Leigh

The company has been based in North Staffordshire since 1962 when the Victoria Theatre Company opened its doors for the first time, becoming the first professional company in Britain to perform permanently in-the-round.

The company's origins go back to the 1950s and Stephen Joseph's Studio Theatre Company, which, from its Scarborough base, toured the country taking the 'theatre' with it – raked platforms providing in-the-round seating for 250. Newcastle-under-Lyme was visited regularly and the converted Victoria cinema finally became a permanent North Staffordshire home.

Under founding Director, Peter Cheeseman, the Victoria Theatre was the company's base for more than 20 years until the New Vic opened in 1986, becoming the first purpose-built theatre-in-the-round in Europe.

The New Vic remains close to its roots and still has a strong relationship with its 'sister-theatre', the Stephen Joseph in Scarborough.

The New Vic Theatre operates thanks to a unique partnership between
Arts Council England, Staffordshire County Council,
Newcastle-under-Lyme Borough Council and Stoke-on-Trent City Council

Cast

Paul Barnhill (DAVE) For the New Vic: *The Bat, East Lynne, Kes, Romeo and Juliet*. Other theatre credits include: *King Cotton* (Lowry and Liverpool Empire); *Antony and Cleopatra, Twelfth Night, Julius Caesar, The Tempest* (Royal Shakespeare Company); *Much Ado About Nothing* (Sheffield Crucible); *Faustus* (Northampton Royal); *The Merchant of Venice, Henry V, A Woman Killed with Kindness* (Northern Broadsides); *Death of a Salesman, The Nativity, All That Trouble That We Had, The Whisper of Angels' Wings* (Birmingham Rep); *Search and Destroy* (New End, Hampstead); *Anna Karenina* (Bolton Octagon); *All's Well That Ends Well* (Nuffield, Southampton); *Tom Jones* (Clwyd Theatr Cymru); *Taking Liberties* (Chester Gateway); *Hamlet* (National Theatre Studio); *Orpheus in the Underworld* (UK tour). In the West End: *Yeoman of the Guard* (Savoy for D'Oyly Carte); *The Pirates of Penzance* (Queen's Theatre); *Die Fledermaus* (Sadler's Wells); RSC Season (Novello). Film and television credits include: *Anorak of Fire, Topsy Turvy* (Thin Man Films); *Holby City, Brookside, Doctors, The Real Arnie Griffen, The Fabulous Bagel Boys, Peak Practice*. Radio credits include: *Edge Falls* (Series I & II), *The Spaceship* (Series I & II), *Beyond the Pole, Beyond the Back of Beyond, Flyfishing, Bloody Rough Holiday Guide, Casualties*.

Tina Gray (BRIDIE) For the New Vic: *On Golden Pond, Once We Were Mothers, A Woman of No Importance, Perfect Days*. Other theatre credits include: *Endgame* (Liverpool Everyman); *The Conservatory* (Old Red Lion); *The History Boys* (NT tour/ West End); *Enjoy, Pygmalion, Habeas Corpus, Noises Off, Bedroom Farce* (York); *A Passionate Woman* (Keswick); *A Day in the Death of Joe Egg, Time of My Life* (Manchester Library); *Relative Values* (Theatre Royal Bath tour); *Anne of Green Gables* (Lilian Baylis); *The Rivals, The Importance of Being Earnest, When I Was a Girl I Used to Scream and Shout, A Nightingale Sang* (Worcester); *Babes in the Wood* (Colchester); *The Glass Menagerie* (Plymouth); *When We Are Married* (West Yorkshire Playhouse); *Jane Eyre* (Clwyd Theatr Cymru); *My Fair Lady* (Cheltenham); *Tess of the D'Urbervilles, Noises Off, Martin Chuzzlewit, Who's Afraid of Virginia Woolf?* (Belgrade, Coventry). Film and television credits include: *Coronation Street, Heartbeat, Doctors, In Suspicious Circumstances, Hotch Potch House, Hiding Place* (BAFTA Award winner). Radio credits include over 1000 plays and readings for the BBC, including: *Agatha Raisin, London Pride, Constance, War with the Newts, The Archers, A Bit of a Hole, Talking to Sticky, Learning to Talk, Dr Finlay, The Piano, No Fond Return of Love, The Vicar of Wakefield*. Tina trained in the Drama Department, Royal Academy of Music, London.

Becky Hindley (SADIE) For the New Vic: *Kitty and Kate*. Other theatre credits include: *Lisa's Sex Strike* (Northern Broadsides, nominated best actress for Manchester Evening News Awards); *Double Death* (The Mill at Sonning); *Mr A's Amazing Maze Plays, Improbable Fiction, Playing God, My Sister Sadie, The Jollies* (Stephen Joseph); *Much Ado About Nothing* (Salisbury Playhouse); *Deathtrap* (No. I Tour for PW Productions); *House and Garden* (Northampton Royal Theatre); *Silly Cow* (Bolton Octagon, nominated best supporting actress for Manchester Evening News Awards); *Comic Potential* (Lyric, West End); *Captain of the Birds* (Abacus Theatre Company); *No Name* (Eastern Angles Theatre Company). Film and television credits include: *Coronation Street, Casualty, Doctors, Holby City, In Deep, The Peter Principle, The Bill, People Like Us*. Radio credits include: *The Duchess of Malfi, Dumb Witness, London Pride, Our Kath, The Remains of the Day, Visiting Time, Life's a Dream, A Town Like Alice*; as well as being a member of the Radio Drama Company.

Tricia Kelly (MARI) This is Tricia's first appearance at the New Vic. Other theatre credits include: *The Adventures of Nicholas Nickleby* (Chichester/UK tour/West End/Toronto); *Unprotected* (Liverpool Everyman/Traverse); *The Maths Tutor* (Hampstead); *Some Explicit Polaroids* (Out of Joint); *Local* (Royal Court Upstairs); *Ion, Julius Caesar* (Royal Shakespeare Company); *Much Ado About Nothing, The Seagull, As You Like It, The Government Inspector* (Sheffield Crucible); *King Lear* (Hackney Empire/West Yorkshire Playhouse); *Sunsets & Glories, Two, Not I* (West Yorkshire Playhouse); *Barbarians, Dancing at Lughnasa, Jamaica Inn* (Salisbury Playhouse); *Victory, The Last Supper, Seven Lears, Golgo* (Wrestling School); *The Whisper of Angels' Wings, Season's Greetings* (Birmingham Rep); *Fen* (Joint Stock/Royal

Court/New York); *A Mouthful of Birds, Deadlines* (Joint Stock/Royal Court); *East Lynne* (Greenwich); *The Voysey Inheritance* (UK tour); *The Choice, The House Under the Stars, The Cassilis Engagement, The Way of the World* (Orange Tree, Richmond); *Juno and the Paycock* (National Theatre). Film and television credits include: *My Family, Casualty, EastEnders, The Bill, High Stakes, Dangerous Lady, The Josie Lawrence Show, B&B, In Sickness and In Health, Christobel, A Small Dance, Top Dog, Big Feet, Real Lies.* After a degree in English and Politics at Lancaster University, Tricia trained as a teacher.

Nicola Sanderson (KATH) This is Nicola's first appearance at the New Vic. Other theatre credits include: *The Man with Two Gaffers* (York Theatre Royal/Northern Broadsides); *A Woman Killed with Kindness, Henry V* (Northern Broadsides); *Fast Food* (Manchester Royal Exchange); *Somewhere* (National Theatre); *Itchy* (National Theatre Studio); *The Servant* (Birmingham Rep); *Bad Company* (The Bush); *Finger Food* (Assembly Rooms, Edinburgh); *Believe Me* (Southwark Playhouse); *Was He Anyone?* (Union); *Confetti* (Oval House/Chelsea Theatre); *Some Leaves Turning* (Young Vic); *Mad/Bad* (Pilot); *National Theatre* (Kings Head); *Lifelines* (Theatre Foundry). Television credits include: *EastEnders, Extras, Coronation Street, Trial and Retribution, Casualty, Mandy Kramer's Drivetime, Where the Heart Is, Family Affairs, William and Mary, A&E, The Bill, Touching Evil, City Central, Forgive and Forget, Peak Practice, The Governor, A Perfect Match, The Peter Principle, Smashie and Nicey, Stop the World, Is This About Crop Circles?, Low Level Panic.* Radio credits include: *Ed Reardon's Week, Mastering the Universe* with Dawn French, four series of *Dave Podmore* (BBC Radio 4).

Creative Team

Deborah McAndrew (Writer) Deborah studied Drama at Manchester University before embarking upon an acting career; which includes extensive work on radio and television, and in touring and repertory theatre. Her adaptation of Leopold Lewis' *The Bells* for Northern Broadsides Theatre Company opened at the Viaduct Theatre, Halifax, in 2004 and toured the UK. Her first original play, *Vacuum*, was also premiered by Northern Broadsides in 2006 prior to touring. *Vacuum* will be produced again in August 2008 by Esk Valley Theatre. Deborah's current commissions include a new adaptation of Dario Fo's *Accidental Death of an Anarchist*, which will be produced by Northern Broadsides in September 2008, and *King Macbeth* for Reveal Theatre Company, which will premiere in Spring 2009. Deborah has spent time on writing attachment at the National Theatre Studio and is currently on writing attachment at Birmingham Repertory Theatre.

Gwenda Hughes (Director) For the New Vic: *The Prime of Miss Jean Brodie, Stags and Hens, Smoke, A Christmas Carol, East Lynne, Dancing at Lughnasa, Pinocchio, Once We Were Mothers, A Woman of No Importance, Four Nights in Knaresborough, Kes, Hector's House, The Beauty Queen of Leenane, Romeo and Juliet, By Jeeves, Toad of Toad Hall, Big Maggie, Who's Afraid of Virginia Woolf?, Moll Flanders, The Wizard of Oz, Office Suite, Broken Glass, She Knows You Know!, Othello, A Passionate Woman, The Tenant of Wildfell Hall.* As Associate Director of Birmingham Rep, over 25 productions including: *The Whisper of Angels' Wings, The Winslow Boy, Loot, Once On This Island* (West End and Olivier Award for Best Musical); over 50 productions for children including, as Artistic Director of Watford Palace TIE, *Taking Liberties, Dirty Rascals, Worlds Apart,* and *Past Caring* with adults and children with learning difficulties. At the Theatre Centre, London: *Billy the Kid, Inside Out, 1983, Face Values* and *Sack of Lies.* Gwenda has worked as a freelance director with New Perspectives Theatre Company, Unicorn, M6, Red Ladder, Women's Theatre Group, The Young Vic, Oldham Coliseum, Lip Service, the NYT and Salisbury Playhouse. She stepped down as Artistic Director of the New Vic in December 2006 to spend more time with her garden. She has been working as a freelance director, writer and researcher, running courses at Birmingham University and Dolphin Dance Studios. She is currently writing a handbook for Directors called *Clocking On at the Play Factory.* Her garden is looking fabulous.

Lis Evans (Designer) As Resident Designer for the New Vic, over 80 productions, including: *Great Expectations* (costume), *Laurel and Hardy, Romeo and Juliet, blue/orange, Jamaica Inn, Oliver!, Stags and Hens, Poor Mrs Pepys, Sizwe Banzi is Dead, The Graduate, Kitty and Kate, Pinocchio, Stepping Out, Amadeus, Kes, Carmen, My Night with Reg, Lonesome West, The Beauty Queen of Leenane, The Railway Children, By Jeeves, Cleo, Camping, Emmanuelle and Dick, Pat and Margaret, Toad of Toad Hall, Top Girls.* Other theatre credits include: *Romeo and Juliet, Vacuum* (Northern Broadsides); *The Tempest* (Northern Broadsides/China tour); design, painting and making for various productions in Nottingham, Manchester, Bradford, Edinburgh and London. Design exhibitions: Cardiff, Stoke, Nottingham, Manchester, Sheffield and London. Lis has contributed to the National Life Stories collection for the British Library Sound Archive. Lis trained at Cardiff Art School and Trent Polytechnic, Nottingham.

Daniella Beattie (Lighting Designer) For the New Vic: *Great Expectations, Laurel and Hardy, Les Liaisons Dangereuses, On Golden Pond, Jamaica Inn, Oliver!, The Prime of Miss Jean Brodie, Stags and Hens, The Safari Party, One Flew Over the Cuckoo's Nest, Smoke, A Christmas Carol, Sizwe Banzi is Dead, As You Like It, East Lynne, The Graduate, Kitty and Kate, Pinocchio, To Kill a Mockingbird, Once We Were Mothers, Can't Pay Won't Pay, Amadeus, Beauty and the Beast, Kes, Carmen, Once a Catholic, The Lonesome West, Love Me Slender, The Duchess of Malfi, The Marriage of Figaro, Outside Edge, The Beauty Queen of Leenane, Pump Boys and Dinettes, Romeo and Juliet, Billy Liar, All That Trouble That We Had, Cleo, Camping, Emmanuelle and Dick, Pat and Margaret, Ham!.* For New Vic Borderlines and Education: *Our Country's Good, Blow the Whistle, Lost, The Caucasian Chalk Circle.* Other theatre credits include: *Romeo and Juliet, The Tempest* (Northern Broadsides/New Vic); *The Mikado* (Orange Tree, Richmond). Daniella has a degree in Theatre Design and Technology from Bretton Hall, University of Leeds.

Peter Morgan (Co-Lighting Designer) This is Peter's first lighting design for the New Vic's main stage. As Deputy Chief Electrician, Pete has worked on over 20 shows at the New Vic, including: *Don Giovanni, Great Expectations, Laurel and Hardy, Romeo and Juliet, Be My Baby* and *The Wizard of Oz.* Re-lighting includes: *Laurel and Hardy* transfer from the New Vic to the Stephen Joseph Theatre, Scarborough. Designs include: *Cuba, The Government Inspector, Nassradim, Summer Showback, Trelawny of the Wells* (New Vic Education); *Pitchfork Disney, Marowitz Hamlet* (Middlesex University). Peter is also the Lighting Designer and Operator for the band, 'Off Rock'. Peter studied Drama and Technical Theatre Studies at Middlesex University.

James Earls-Davis (Sound Designer) For the New Vic, all main house sound designs since 1987, including: *Don Giovanni, Great Expectations, Laurel and Hardy, Be My Baby, Cider with Rosie, Les Liaisons Dangereuses, Jamaica Inn, The Glee Club, Oliver!, One Flew Over the Cuckoo's Nest, Abigail's Party, A Christmas Carol, Sizwe Banzi is Dead, As You Like It, Four Nights in Knaresborough, Carmen.* Original music includes: *blue/orange, Misery, Dealer's Choice, Romeo and Juliet, Broken Glass* (solo); *Smoke, Once We Were Mothers, Kes, All That Trouble That We Had* (with Russell Gregory); *Romeo and Juliet* (with Sue Moffat). Sound design and/or original music includes: *Rebecca, Frozen* (Theatre by the Lake); *Homefront, Sticks and Stones* (Reveal Theatre Company); *Twelfth Night* (Belgrade); *Her Big Chance* (Harrogate). Several sound designs and/or original music for New Vic Borderlines and Education projects; soundtracks for community arts projects and films. James is bass player in improv/noise band 'Flight of the Dobermen'.

Mark Langley (Voice Coach) For the New Vic: *Great Expectations, The Wizard of Oz, Jamaica Inn, The Glee Club, The Prime of Miss Jean Brodie, The Safari Party, Poor Mrs Pepys, One Flew Over the Cuckoo's Nest, Sizwe Banzi is Dead, Dancing at Lughnasa, Kitty and Kate, To Kill a Mockingbird, A Woman of No Importance, Perfect Days, Beauty and the Beast, Kes, East is East, The Lonesome West, Blue Remembered Hills, Big Maggie, Top Girls, Cleo, Camping, Emmanuelle and Dick, Billy Liar.* Other theatre credits include: *All the Ordinary Angels, Mary Barton* (Royal Exchange, Manchester). Television and film credits include: *Early Doors* (BBC2); *Dead Clever* (Granada). Mark is General Manager of The Arden, Manchester, and works nationally and internationally as a freelance voice coach. He has worked on productions for the West Yorkshire Playhouse, the Crucible Theatre, Opera North and for productions staged at the Royal National Theatre and in the West End. Mark trained at Saint John's College, York.

New Vic Theatre Staff

FLAMINGOLAND

Deborah McAndrew

Characters

MARI, *fifty-eight*

BRIDIE, *sixty-five*

KATHLEEN, *thirty-eight*

SADIE, *forty*

DAVE, *thirty-four*

All characters speak with a Yorkshire accent.

Time: the present, or the recent past.

Dialogue in [square brackets] is intention, not to be spoken.

This text went to press before the end of rehearsals and so may differ slightly from the play as performed.

PROLOGUE

In an isolated space on the stage, a single spot lights SADIE, *who begins to play a banjo. The music starts slowly and builds to a joyful, fast-paced crescendo.*

Snap light change to:

ACT ONE

Living room of a modest house in a small Yorkshire town. Sparsely furnished – sofa, armchair, sideboard, coffee table, television. Stacked apple boxes, labelled: 'ST DAVID'S', 'CAR-BOOT', 'BRIDIE', 'SADIE', 'KATHLEEN'. Exit to hall and front door. Stairs directly from living room to bedrooms and loft.

Opening to a half-visible kitchen, with yellow Post-it notes dotting the various cupboards and objects. The kitchen leads to a back door and garden.

MARI *sits on the floor by a home paper-shredder, a mountain of shreds beside her. She works through a pile of papers, methodically shredding some and placing others aside in an unlabelled cardboard box.* MARI *wears a wig.*

KATHLEEN *enters through the front door, laden with two bags of groceries. She is a curvy woman, dressed in the uniform of a bank or building society.*

MARI (*observing the bags*). God help me.

> KATHLEEN *dumps the bags and exits, returning moments later with another bag and a cheap bunch of pink flowers, which* MARI *clocks disapprovingly.*

KATHLEEN. Brighten the place up.

She heads straight through to the kitchen, returning promptly to hang her coat by the front door.

What's all that?

MARI. All what?

KATHLEEN. Stuck on the cupboards.

MARI. Organisation.
So we know what's going where.

KATHLEEN. You could write me a list.

MARI. That's my system.

KATHLEEN. Why don't you leave it to me?

MARI. When?

KATHLEEN. Later.

MARI. After.

KATHLEEN. I don't mind shouldering the burden.

MARI. My life. My burden.

KATHLEEN *exits to the kitchen. We catch glimpses of her through the opening.*

(*Calling.*) Anyway, with the best will, you might not get it right. You'll be under pressure.

KATHLEEN. There's hardly much.

MARI. There won't be anything.

MARI *picks through the documents; reading briefly, shredding, putting to one side.*

Ha! 'Stainless steel.'
Lifetime guarantee.

KATHLEEN *enters with the flowers, which have been inartistically plonked in a gaudy yellow vase.*

I say, Kathleen – that's funny.
I've the guarantee here for my pans.
Lifetime.

Never mind Omega 3 – what you need for longevity is a
copper bottom.
You're having them.
There's a Post-it on the stockpot.

She slips the guarantee into the box marked 'KATHLEEN'.

Just remember, though, if they go wrong, tell them you
bought them yourself. I don't know if they're guaranteed for
two lifetimes –
Might be a legal loophole.

KATHLEEN. Where should I put these?

MARI glares at the flowers.

I know pink doesn't go in yellow, but I couldn't find another
vase.

MARI. Where's the note I put on it?

KATHLEEN. What? I don't know.
Fell off in the cupboard.

MARI. Find it. I don't want any confusion.
That vase is going to your Auntie Bridie.

KATHLEEN. I'll remember.

MARI. Will you, though?
Will you?
What if you're muddled by grief?

KATHLEEN. I'll try not to be.

MARI. Get the note, please, Kathleen.

*KATHLEEN puts the vase down on the sideboard and exits
to the kitchen.*

(*Calling.*) I hope you've remembered what I said about flowers.

KATHLEEN returns with the Post-it.

Did you hear that?
No flowers.

KATHLEEN. You said.

MARI. I don't want any.

KATHLEEN. I know.

MARI. Don't be getting it into your head to surprise me.
You won't surprise me.
I'll be dead.

KATHLEEN *sticks the note to the vase. The note says
'Bridie'.*

KATHLEEN. Does Bridie like this vase?

MARI. Course she does.

KATHLEEN. I don't think she likes it.
It's a bit bright.

MARI. Our Bridie has always admired that vase.
It's me that doesn't like it.

KATHLEEN. Well, if Bridie likes it and you don't, why didn't
you give her it before now?

MARI. That vase belonged to my mother.
I treasure it.
It's hideous, but what can you do?
Now Bridie will have to treasure it an' all.

KATHLEEN. You know she doesn't like it.

MARI. What I know is that when we cleared out Mam's place,
Bridie picked everything over and was gracious enough to
leave that 'gorgeous' vase for me to have. It was Mam's
favourite. I couldn't throw it out or give it away, so I have
endured it for twenty-five years.
Now it's Bridie's turn.

KATHLEEN. It's cheerful.
Optimistic.
That'll be why you don't like it.
I suppose it must be quite old. Might be worth something.

MARI. If Bridie's heartless enough to sell it for a profit, that's
between her and her conscience.

KATHLEEN. I hope you've not left me anything ugly.

MARI. You've got stuff you'll use.
  The pans and the wine glasses.

KATHLEEN. Save me swigging it out of the bottle.

MARI. Maybe you'll learn to cook.

KATHLEEN. I can cook.

MARI. Microwave moussaka isn't food, Kathleen.

KATHLEEN. I thought it'd be convenient for you.
  You said you were tired.

MARI. That was the tablets.

KATHLEEN. And we're not repeating that little drama, are we?

  MARI *ignores this and begins to shred again.* KATHLEEN
  returns to the kitchen to put the shopping away.

MARI (*calling*). Did you get bin bags?

KATHLEEN (*from the kitchen*). What?

MARI. Bin bags.

KATHLEEN (*from the kitchen*). What?

MARI. Bin bags!

KATHLEEN (*appearing with a new roll of bin bags*). You could
  have recycled all that, you know.

MARI. Oh no.
  Identity theft.
  It's the latest thing.
  They come in the night, like foxes, raiding your bins.

KATHLEEN. Are there many fifty-eight-year-old women
  looking for new identities?

MARI. You'd be surprised.

KATHLEEN. Wouldn't matter to you anyway.

MARI. You don't know that. I might be able to look down and
  see some vixen pretending to be me. Living it up with my
  National Insurance number.

KATHLEEN (*heading back to the kitchen*). I wouldn't worry, nobody'd believe that was you.

MARI. I'll take my name with me, thank you.

MARI *tears off a bag and begins tidying up the shredded papers.* KATHLEEN *enters from the kitchen with her purse.*

KATHLEEN. I've got your change.

MARI. I don't want it.

KATHLEEN. Here you are.

MARI. You have it.

KATHLEEN. What is the point of me trying to save you money?

MARI. I only gave you twenty.

KATHLEEN. I got the offers.

MARI. I don't want it.

KATHLEEN. One pound sixty.

MARI. Buy yourself a coffee.

KATHLEEN (*giving up*). You'll get steak next time.

MARI. I won't eat it.

KATHLEEN. Sirloin.

MARI. Can't get it down.

KATHLEEN. Do you good. Iron.

MARI. Can't digest it.

KATHLEEN. Liver then.

MARI. Offal.

KATHLEEN. It's quite dear, you know. Offal's not peasant food any more. They have it in all the poshest restaurants now.

MARI. And who takes you to posh restaurants?

KATHLEEN. I've had all kinds of things.
Heart, kidney, sweetbreads.

Lamb's liver – sautéd with baby shallots and garlic, in a port and redcurrant gravy.

MARI. If only you'd show that kind of respect to your own liver.

The doorbell rings. MARI *continues tidying.* KATHLEEN *goes to answer the door. As she greets the visitor, her voice changes pitch – higher and warmer.*

KATHLEEN (*off*). Hello.

DAVE (*off*). Environmental health.

KATHLEEN (*off*). Oh. Come in.

MARI (*calling*). Is that you, Dave?

KATHLEEN *enters with* DAVE.

DAVE. Now then, Mari. We got any this morning?

MARI. Haven't heard anything.

DAVE. I'll have a nosey, then, shall I?

MARI. You know where it is.

DAVE. Righto.

DAVE *exits upstairs.*

KATHLEEN (*approving*). That's your man, is it?

MARI. He's not my man.

KATHLEEN. How many times is that now?

MARI. Only twice.

KATHLEEN. What do you do? Put monkey nuts in the guttering to tempt them in?

MARI. They reckon to have blocked it up last time. It's not my fault.
Have you ever seen one close up?

KATHLEEN. Can't say I have.

MARI. They're not cute, you know.
Not really.

You see 'em, running about the garden, washing their noses,
and you think they're God's creatures.
But they're not.

KATHLEEN. I thought we all were.

MARI. Rats.
Rats with fluffy tails.
And you mustn't forget that.
Mustn't get sentimental.
Dave shoots 'em.
It's the most humane way.
Though I think it affects him. He's sensitive.

KATHLEEN. Is he?

MARI. And you can get that tone out of your voice.

KATHLEEN. What tone?

MARI. Stretching, breathless, like you've just woken up.
He's a married man.

KATHLEEN. I thought you said he was divorced.

MARI. I believe that's what they call it.
And don't think I don't know the ways of the world. Doesn't
change anything. Adultery's adultery, whichever way you
slice and butter it. There's a chance of a reconciliation with
his wife. He doesn't need a woman like you –

KATHLEEN. Like what?
Wanton? Easy?

MARI. Lonely.

Beat.

KATHLEEN. Does he have a cup of tea, your Dave?

MARI. He does – and I'll be making it for him.
See if I can't rustle up a Garibaldi.

MARI *exits to the kitchen.* DAVE *comes downstairs carrying
a squirrel trap, covered with a nasty old cloth.*

DAVE. There's babies.

KATHLEEN. Is there?

DAVE. Got the male here. Big 'un.
   Do you want to have a look?

KATHLEEN. Are you going to shoot him?

DAVE. He won't feel anything.

KATHLEEN. No, thanks.

DAVE. Shan't go near the dray till we've got the female,
   though.
   Wouldn't dare.
   I've seen some nasty injuries.

KATHLEEN. Do they attack?

DAVE. My mate, Sam, who I work with, he has two finger ends
   missing. (*Holding up two fingers.*) These two. Like King
   Henry's archers.

KATHLEEN. And a squirrel bit them off?

DAVE. Oh, no. Somebody slammed a car door on him when he
   was a kid. Actually, they were more crushed than severed.
   He tells it better than me. It's a talking point when you're
   first getting to know him. 'Digitally challenged' – that's what
   he calls it.
   Still goes fishing, though.
   You must be Kathleen.

KATHLEEN. Yes.

DAVE. Mari's told me all about you. Proud of you, she is.
   Says you're very good to her.

KATHLEEN. Mum's making you a cup of tea. And a Garibaldi.

DAVE. I'll just pop Tufty in the van.

   DAVE *exits via the front door.* MARI *appears in the kitchen
   doorway.*

MARI. He got one, then?

KATHLEEN. The male.

MARI. Daft bugger.

> MARI *turns back into the kitchen.* KATHLEEN *loosens the top button of her blouse and runs a hand through her hair.*

(*Calling from the kitchen.*) You want a drink, Kath?

KATHLEEN. No, ta.

> DAVE *re-enters.* MARI *comes through from the kitchen carrying a mug, labelled with a Post-it note that reads: 'St David's'.*

MARI (*handing the mug to* DAVE). Can't find the Garibaldis.

DAVE. Ta.

> MARI *clocks* KATHLEEN's *blouse.*

MARI. There's all sorts of peculiar stuff in my cupboards since our Kathleen's been doing my shopping.
Last week I nearly starved to death.

KATHLEEN. How could you starve with a fridge full of food?

MARI. Not an edible thing in. She'd bought me these sausages – well, I don't know what they were – some manner of foreign.

KATHLEEN. Cumberland.

MARI. Garlic!
I took the cellophane off – stink nearly knocked me out.

KATHLEEN. They were – [English sausages.]

MARI. She knows I don't like garlic.

KATHLEEN. The packet had a picture of a Penrith pig on it.

MARI. You have to be vigilant. Read the label. Garlic is insidious.

DAVE. It's a strong flavour.

MARI. It's not a flavour, it's an odour.
A rank odour.
Doesn't have to be much, but I know.

KATHLEEN. She can smell France from here.

MARI (*exiting to the kitchen*). Are you feeling warm, Kathleen?

KATHLEEN*'s hand lifts involuntarily to her loosened button.*

KATHLEEN. Does your mother give you this much trouble, Dave?

DAVE. My mother died.

KATHLEEN. Sorry.

DAVE. S'all right.
Later on, in my teens, I had a stepmother.
Like Snow White.

MARI (*calling from the kitchen*). Battenburg!

KATHLEEN (*calling to* MARI). You like Battenburg.

MARI (*appearing in doorway*). No, I don't.

DAVE. I do.

MARI. Tastes of arsenic.

KATHLEEN. You like Bakewells.

MARI. That's English arsenic.

DAVE. Garibaldi was Italian.

MARI. I'll get the knife.

DAVE *takes a swig of his tea and notices the Post-it: 'St David's'.*

DAVE. What's this?

MARI *returns with cake, plates and knife.*

I say, Mari – 'St David's'! Didn't know you had such a high opinion of me.

KATHLEEN. She thinks you're divine.

MARI. That's the hospice.
How big a piece do you want?

DAVE. Just normal.

MARI *dishes out the cake*.

Been quiet lately.
You're the only squirrel.
Apart from that, I've only seen half-a-dozen cockroaches
and a dead cat for the best part of a week.

MARI. Well – this area is coming up, you know.
I noticed the other day – there's a house lower down has con-
crete balls on the gate.

DAVE. She's having block paving.

MARI. And who's paying for that?

DAVE. Muggins.

MARI. Did you see the kiddies at the weekend?

DAVE. I did – but she pulled the rug.
Lauren had to go to a friend's birthday party at two o'clock.
Only she wouldn't even let me take her – wouldn't tell me
where, you know.
I had to have her back home by one to get ready – only had
her for three hours. And it grounded me with Jess an' all. I'd
planned to take them to Aqua Planet, but it was too far. Had
to make do with Chunky Monkeys.
Didn't tell me till I got there.
Could have warned me in advance.
Could have changed to Sunday then, but no.
She knew I'd have something planned.
Sabotaged me.
Sabotage.

MARI. Dave's wife is a domineering woman.

DAVE. Ex-wife.

MARI. It's a problem when women wear the trousers. Men get
undermined. Emasculated.

DAVE. She's fleeced me, I know that.

MARI. I keep telling Kathleen. Men need gentle handling.
She'll always be on her own while she's so bossy.

KATHLEEN. Perhaps I choose to live alone.

MARI. Makes no odds now anyway. You're too old for kiddies.

KATHLEEN. How old are your children, Dave?

DAVE. Lauren's eight and Jessica's five.
    They're good girls. I wouldn't be without 'em.
    Lauren was a bit of a surprise, you know.
    That's why we got married.
    Jess wasn't far off a miracle.

MARI. All babies are miracles, Dave.

DAVE. Are they? Then I'll tell you what, Mari – it's like the ten
    plagues of Egypt in your loft.

MARI. How many do you think?

DAVE. Counted at least five.

MARI. Goners.

DAVE. Once I've got the mother, I'll fetch the gun and shoot
    them on sight. They shouldn't be moving too fast yet and I'll
    just pick them off easily.

KATHLEEN. Oh, very nice.

MARI. What's up with you, all of a sudden?

DAVE. It's more humane. Less stress for them than trapping,
    taking them away and then shooting them.

KATHLEEN. I'm so glad for them.

MARI. People don't have better deaths.

    Beat.

KATHLEEN. I'll have that tea now, Mam.

    MARI *exits to the kitchen.* KATHLEEN *watches* DAVE
    enjoy his cake.

DAVE. Mmm.
    I love marzipan.

KATHLEEN. Do you?

DAVE. It's originally from Persia, you know.
That's modern-day Iran.
In olden times it was a great luxury.

KATHLEEN. You're an expert.

DAVE. Not really.
I have this sort of brain that collects facts – soaked up as I go along. I read a lot of cereal packets.

KATHLEEN. So, what else do you know?

DAVE. About marzipan?
Once upon a time only the very rich ate it.
Poor weren't allowed.
It's very sensual – with its intoxicating almond perfume.
It was believed it inflamed the passions.

DAVE gives her a wink.

KATHLEEN. And you learned all that from a cereal packet?
I'll have to stop skipping breakfast.

DAVE. Most important meal of the day.

KATHLEEN. Not just flakes and Grape-Nuts.

DAVE. Rolled oats – they're the best.

BRIDIE (*off*). Hello! Hello!

BRIDIE enters in a rush.

I've let myself in.

She sees DAVE and KATHLEEN.

Oh no. Oh no. Where is she?
No!
Tell me she isn't.
Tell me she isn't.

MARI (*returning from the kitchen with KATHLEEN's tea*). She isn't.

BRIDIE. Mari! God above!

MARI. I believe so.

BRIDIE. I ran into Jean in Sunny Climes. She said there'd been some awful mix-up with your tablets and you weren't at mass. I've rushed straight over. Frightened me to death.

MARI. Apparently.

BRIDIE. Figure of speech, Mari.

MARI. On your way, Dave. Don't let us keep you.

BRIDIE. Hello, Dave.

DAVE. How are you, Bridie?

BRIDIE. I'll be all right when I get my breath.
Gave me a nasty turn, seeing your van outside.
Environmental health.
Thought perhaps she'd not been discovered.
Gone off, you know.

MARI. Do you know each other?

BRIDIE. Only professionally.

Dave did our rat.

MARI (*jealous*). When did you have a rat?

DAVE. Common problem.
They were laying new pipes and disturbed a nest.
I had a number of calls to sightings of single rats that week.

BRIDIE. Marvellous, he is. Like the Pied Piper.

MARI. Then I hope you paid him, or he'll be back for your children.

DAVE. How is Sadie?

BRIDIE. Same as ever.

DAVE. Still living in that flat down Station Road?

BRIDIE. She seems to like it there – God knows why.
She's a perfectly good room at home.
I'm having the kitchen done.

DAVE. I see her sometimes. In The Lamb and Flag.

BRIDIE. Who, our Sadie?
  That's like a bikers' pub, isn't it?

DAVE. Sort of, but they have bands on.

BRIDIE. Bands?

DAVE. Folk, old fashioned R and B –

BRIDIE. You must be thinking of somewhere else.
  Our Sadie likes a quiet place.

MARI. Where is it you go drinking, Kathleen?

KATHLEEN. Cock and Bull.

BRIDIE. I'll say hello to her for you.

DAVE. Right. I'll push off.
  I'll just pop a new trap up there for you, Mari, and close the
  ladder.

MARI. Okay.

  DAVE *exits via the front door.*

BRIDIE. Now then, our Mari. What's been going on?

MARI. There's tea in the pot.

BRIDIE. I'll have a coffee.

  This is typical BRIDIE *contrariness, but* MARI *exits
  stoically to make her a coffee.*

  So, what was it? Jean said overdose.

KATHLEEN. Underdose. She thinks some of the tablets make
  her drowsy, so she decided for herself how many she should
  be taking.

BRIDIE. And do they? Make her drowsy?

KATHLEEN. Probably, they're for the pain.
  Got herself in a state, thought she was in her last agony and
  called an ambulance.

BRIDIE. Why wasn't I informed?

KATHLEEN. It only happened on Saturday. They didn't even keep her in overnight. Just sorted out her dosage and sent her home. She's fine.

BRIDIE. I should be informed.

KATHLEEN. If there was anything to tell.

BRIDIE. How would you like it?

KATHLEEN. I can't help gossip.

BRIDIE. Hearing your sister's overdosed in the queue for the bureau de change.

DAVE *enters with an empty trap and proceeds directly upstairs.*

KATHLEEN. Where you off to?

BRIDIE. Barcelona.

KATHLEEN. Nice.

BRIDIE. Not for long. Just a weekend city break, you know. Take me out of myself.

MARI (*returning with* BRIDIE's *coffee*). I've made it too milky.

BRIDIE. It'll be fine.

MARI. Came out a bit fast.

BRIDIE. Hot and wet.

MARI. No, I'm sure it's too milky.

BRIDIE (*taking the cup*). I'm gasping, Mari, it won't touch the sides.

MARI. You don't like it milky.

BRIDIE (*taking a sip*). It's fine.

MARI. It's claggy.

BRIDIE. It's not.

MARI. You like it strong.

She swipes the cup from BRIDIE.

I'll pour some away.

MARI *exits to the kitchen with the coffee.*

BRIDIE (*calling*). I'll have a sugar in it then, Mari.
For the shock.

KATHLEEN. Who you off to Spain with, Bridie?

BRIDIE. Sadie. It was her idea. Thought it'd take me out of
myself, what with – you know.

KATHLEEN. I could do with a bit of that.

BRIDIE. You're bearing up, Kathy.

KATHLEEN. Well, to be honest –

BRIDIE. I was only saying to our Sadie last night, how well
you're bearing up.
'She's a soldier, is our Kathy.'
It's always a strain on an only child. Pity, really. I'm sure
you'd have had brothers and sisters if your father hadn't run
off when he did.

MARI (*returning with coffee*). Here you are, Bridie.

BRIDIE. Just leave it on the table.
Now I've got my breath, I'll nip out for a ciggie.

BRIDIE *exits via the front door.* MARI *places the mug on
the coffee table.*

MARI (*with satisfaction*). It'll go cold.

MARI *sits, visibly tired.* DAVE *comes downstairs.*

DAVE. All done.

MARI. Right, love.

DAVE. I'll be back to check same time tomorrow.

MARI. That'll do.

DAVE. Nice to meet you, Kathleen.

KATHLEEN. And you.

DAVE. And remember what I said about breakfast.

DAVE exits.

MARI. Cut me a slice of that cake, Kathleen.

KATHLEEN. You don't like it.

MARI. Beggars can't be choosers.

KATHLEEN (*cutting the cake*). Sadie's taking Bridie to Barcelona.

MARI. How long for?

KATHLEEN. Weekend.

MARI. I'll make sure I don't die while they're away.

KATHLEEN hands her a slab of cake.

For heaven's sake, Kathleen, I can't manage all that.

KATHLEEN halves the portion and eats one half herself.
MARI bites into her cake.

Oh no. I can't eat that.
Too almondy.
Bitter.
Why couldn't you just get Fondant Fancies?

KATHLEEN. I will, next time.

MARI. Get them for the funeral.

KATHLEEN. What?

MARI. Make a note.
Go on. We haven't done the wake yet.

KATHLEEN. But you've said – there'll only be me and Bridie and Sadie.

MARI. So?

KATHLEEN. So – well, I don't suppose I've given it much thought, but if I had… I expect we'll all just go for a pub lunch or something.

Long beat.

MARI. Get the book, Kathleen.

KATHLEEN. Where is it?

MARI. On the top of the boxes.

KATHLEEN. No, it isn't.

MARI. In between.

> KATHLEEN *retrieves a black notepad from between two of the boxes. She then sits and finds a clean page.*

KATHLEEN. What do you want me to write?

MARI. Wake. Food.
Ham sandwiches. Crisps. Pork pie. Fondant Fancies.
Tea. Coffee.

> KATHLEEN *writes.*

Don't need too much.

KATHLEEN. You won't be able to stop other people coming, you know.

MARI. And I suppose you'll disobey my dying wishes.
I've left money for a mass. Anybody else can go to that.
Not one of them has been to see me since I've had to stop work.

KATHLEEN. Perhaps they just don't know what to say.

MARI. They have plenty to say *about* me – to our Bridie in the town. Tattling. Why can't they come round here to gossip? At least while they're here I'll know they're not talking about me.

KATHLEEN. I'm sure they're not talking about you.

MARI. So how did Jean know about my pills?

KATHLEEN. I expect Father Donal told her.

MARI. He's altogether too loose, is that Donal. He brought me communion the other day and he muttered something about making peace with God – 'whatever you conceive him to be'. Fancy a Catholic priest saying that. It's let me down, has the Church. Let me down badly. I've lived a life of denial

and discipline. Discipline and denial. That's how I was
brought up. What they insisted on. And now they've gone all
cuddly. Blurred at the edges.
It's confusing.
Am I going through the narrow gate, or aren't I?
I'll tell you what, if I'm not... Well, I don't want to hear it.

KATHLEEN. Does it matter what Donal or anyone else says?
You know what you know.

MARI. Do I? Do I? When I look around, at the world; and
when I look back...

KATHLEEN. You shouldn't look back. You'll turn into a pillar
of salt.

BRIDIE *enters*.

BRIDIE. Human again.

MARI. Your coffee's cold.

BRIDIE. No mind. Ooh, is that Battenburg?
(*Helping herself to cake*.) I'll skidaddle in a min. Now I
know you're all right.

MARI. We're just discussing the funeral.

BRIDIE. Why? Who's died?
(*Realising*.) Oh, Mari.

MARI. I'm not leaving it to the last minute.

BRIDIE. You'll want to chose the hymns, I suppose.
Just so long as you don't expect me or Sadie to sing.

KATHLEEN. I'm not singing on my own.

BRIDIE. What?

KATHLEEN. There's only the three of us invited.

BRIDIE. I didn't realise people were 'invited' to a funeral.

MARI. Who else is there?

BRIDIE. What about your dad, Kathy?

MARI. I don't want him there.

KATHLEEN. We don't know where he is.
I'm not bothered.

BRIDIE. What about all your church friends – Jean and Sheila
and all those others?

MARI. They're not close. It's a private thing.

KATHLEEN. So – just me, you and Sadie.

BRIDIE. Won't be much of a wake.

KATHLEEN (*reading from the book*). And that'll be back here
with ham sandwiches, crisps, pork pie and Fondant Fancies.

MARI. Funerals are for the living.

BRIDIE. You might be looking down on us.

MARI. I might not.

BRIDIE. You're the one who believes –

MARI. I expect we pass on somewhere, but who's to say we
can see what's going on behind our backs?

BRIDIE. What hymns have you chosen?

KATHLEEN (*reading*). 'The Lord's My Shepherd' –

MARI. Crimmond.

KATHLEEN. 'O Mother Most Pure' and 'Sweet Sacrament
Divine'.

BRIDIE. That goes very high.

MARI. I expect you to sing, Bridie –

BRIDIE. Well, I suppose if God gave me a lousy voice, He
can't grumble –

MARI. And Sadie too.

BRIDIE. Not Sadie. She's worse than me.

MARI. How would you know?

BRIDIE. Because I taught her her nursery rhymes – and I'm
telling you, that little pixie singing 'Humpty Dumpty' was a
sound only a mother could love.

MARI. You gave her no encouragement.

BRIDIE. I gave her all the encouragement I could, but what can you do? No point giving them false delusions.

MARI. She could have learned an instrument.

BRIDIE. And I had money to throw away on expensive music lessons.
Anyway, to play an instrument you have to have an ear for it. Our Sadie is tone deaf.

MARI. Well, then – when you and her are singing 'O Mother Most Pure', I'll have at least one reason to be glad I'm dead.

BRIDIE. Kathleen, can't you talk some sense into her? Stop this morbidity. And what's with all these shreds and stickers?

MARI. It's my system.

BRIDIE. It's a fire trap.
What's in the boxes?

MARI. Never you mind, yet.

KATHLEEN. But don't build your hopes up.
I've got the guarantee for the copper-bottomed pans.

BRIDIE (*clocking the vase*). Oh my God! Am I getting that?

KATHLEEN. Anything that won't go through the shredder.

MARI. That business with my pills – woke me up. So I'm getting organised.

BRIDIE. Why don't you just make a will?

MARI. Because I don't trust the law.
Besides – my life can't be disposed of like that.

BRIDIE. Put your affairs in order, Mari, by all means – but this labelling and that, it's… Well, it's wallowing, that's what it is.

MARI. I'm still strong.
I can make sure everything is as I want it.
I'm depending on the painkillers more and more to get through the day. Before long, I won't be much more than a puddle of morphine –

Then what?
Do you think I'm ready?
When we're born we have nothing.
Not a stick of furniture, or a gas bill, or a bank book.
We don't feel hope or fear or guilt.
We haven't done any deals with life.
Then, bit by bit, we start making a mess all over the place.
Complications, compromises, stuff.
I'm not ready to go back into the dark, but I'm trying.
Preparing, paring.
By the time I have to go I'll have polished my own coffin.

KATHLEEN (*reading*). The Stanford. Oak finish, brass-plated fittings. Inscription plate. Complimentary taffeta interior.

MARI. Booked and paid for.

BRIDIE. Jesus.

MARI. Don't blaspheme, Bridget.

BRIDIE. Well, for God's sake, Mari, what do you expect?

MARI. I expect you'd have liked to choose it for me.

BRIDIE. You're not dead yet.

MARI. No, I'm not.
So make the most of me.

BRIDIE. I mean, you should be thinking about life – when your time's short.

MARI. I am thinking about life. All my life.
What I've had, what I've lost and what I've never had.
I start to see all the walls.
Bricked up – that's me. Like St Julian. Bricked up – inside and out.
Could I have done anything?
Achieved anything – if I hadn't expected nothing of myself?
I don't know, do I?
And now I'll never know.
I'll be just another brief, unremarkable flicker of life.
Born, took a breath of air, and died.
Nothing.

BRIDIE. Not to us, Mari – to us you're a sister, a mother, an auntie.

Long beat as MARI *and* BRIDIE *eyeball each other.*

MARI. Don't worry, Bridie. I'll be tidy.

Beat. BRIDIE *checks her watch.*

Before you go, I have something to ask you.

BRIDIE. Anything, Mari, you know that.

MARI. What are you going to say at my funeral?

BRIDIE. What?

MARI. There'll only be the three of you and you're all going to say a few words. Only, I want to know beforehand what you're going to say.
You don't have to tell me right now. You'll need to give it some thought.

BRIDIE. What do you make of this, Kathy?

KATHLEEN. Already done mine.

MARI. We've been working on it together.
I'll need to hear all three speeches.
Make sure there's no repetition.

BRIDIE. What would I say? I'm not a speaker.

MARI. It doesn't have to be anything profound.

BRIDIE. I don't think I could –

MARI (*sharp*). Is it too much to ask?

BRIDIE. I suppose there's some lovely poems –

MARI (*emotional*). No!
No, Bridie.
I want to hear your words – your own words.
Your own words.
And nothing cosy.

BRIDIE. Right. All right, Mari.

MARI. And Sadie too. You tell her.
  You can manage that.

BRIDIE. I can. I will.

MARI. Off you go, then. You've a bus to catch.

BRIDIE. Yes.
  I'll drop by at the end of the week.
  Ring me if you need anything.

MARI. I will.

BRIDIE exits. KATHLEEN begins to tidy up. MARI stands, motionless and tired. KATHLEEN exits to the kitchen with the dishes.

KATHLEEN returns.

'The family is the original cell of social life.'
That's what it says in the catechism.
'The original cell.'

Banjo music plays.

End of Act One.

ACT TWO

A week later.

The same.

The sofa and coffee table have gone. There are now just three apple boxes, stacked to one side, labelled 'KATHLEEN', 'SADIE', 'BRIDIE'. The armchair, now centre, faces the television, which is on low. Candle and box of matches on top of the television. Funeral notebook on top of the boxes.

MARI *sits alone, a plate on the floor beside her with an untouched sandwich.*

Doorbell.

Beat.

Doorbell.

MARI *rises and exits to the front door.*

MARI (*off*). Come in, love.

DAVE (off). Ta.
    How's things?

MARI (*off*). Much the same and getting worse.

    DAVE *and* MARI *enter.*

    I haven't heard anything this morning.

DAVE. Still? She's a tricky one, is mother. The male was no trouble.

MARI. Perhaps females aren't so daft.

DAVE. You'll be right there, Mari.
    Oh – you're just having your lunch. Sorry.

MARI. I made it too early and didn't really want it.
    Gone a bit curly now.

DAVE. You carry on.

MARI. Have you had anything?

DAVE. Not yet.

MARI. Would you like me to make you a bit of something? I've
plenty in.
Do you like poloni?

DAVE. I'm all right, thank you, Mari.
I fixed my snap this morning. I've a Tupperware in the van.

MARI. What you got?

DAVE. Cheese and pickle.

MARI. My favourite.

DAVE. Just a smear of pickle, you know. The missus always
put a bit too much on when she used to do them. She's sort
of heavy-handed with food. There's a bright side, even to
divorce – at least I get my sarnies made up right.

MARI. You must have loved her once.

DAVE. No. Not really.
We more got caught up together.
I know a lot of men like big women, but she was never really
my type. I like small, dark-haired women.
And uniforms.
Not policewomen – they tend to be tall.
Air hostesses.
Chinese air hostesses.
I've always fancied Chinese women.
Even the ugly ones.

Beat.

You been watching telly?

MARI. A bit.

She goes to switch it off.

I was just watching this geography programme about deserts.
It was interesting.
Flash floods. They pour down from the mountains and make

rivers for just a day or so. I liked the look of it, all this bone-dry sand licked up by the sudden water, slurping and thickening. Then grass just springs up out of nowhere. It's amazing, really. You'd think there'd be no life there, but it's sleeping – waiting. I liked it. Living things can survive for decades on one flood.
You feel like death is relentless, but life is too. It'll find its way somehow. Growing through the cracks in the wall.

DAVE. I like geography. History too. I wasn't any good at school, though. I was one of those kids that education is wasted on.

MARI. You're a clever lad.

DAVE *shrugs*.

You are. You remember all kinds of things.

DAVE. I only remember what I like; what interests me. Remembering stuff that you find boring – that's clever. That's the difference.

MARI. What kind of boring?

DAVE. I don't know – ancient Greek, computer programming, soil.

MARI. Perhaps the people who programme computers wouldn't be able to remember something like the history of marzipan.

DAVE *is strangely discomfited*.

DAVE. I'd better crack on.
Check the trap, and if we've got her, I can start picking off the babies.

MARI. Don't you ever feel sorry for them?

DAVE. I used to.

MARI. Not any more.

DAVE. Not while I'm doing it.

MARI. But, after?

DAVE. No.
But since me and the wife…

MARI. Oh yes?

DAVE. It's daft, really.

MARI. What is?

DAVE. Nah.

MARI. What is?

DAVE. I've not told anyone.

MARI. Tell me.

DAVE. It's just a recurring dream I have.
It's to do with stress, I expect.

MARI. Go on. I'm good with dreams.

DAVE. I'm in this big house, bit like those up Sandy Lane, and
I'm looking for squirrels in the loft. I can hear 'em moving
about, but I can't see 'em. They're gnawing somewhere;
gnawing on something and I can't see. Then all of a sudden I
look down and it's there, chewing on my leg. It's already
chewed it to the bone and the sound I can hear is the
squirrel's teeth champing on my own shinbone.
I scream out and everything goes black and the gnawing gets
louder and louder. Then I stumble forward and I can feel a
crunching under my feet, and in the darkness I start to make
out millions of little bones, stretching out as far as the eye
can see. As I watch, these little bones twitch and rattle and
start to join together to make skeleton squirrels. All the squirrels I've ever killed, coming back to life, growing flesh and
fur on their tiny bones. Hundreds. Thousands. Then they all
turn together and stare at me, with savagery and revenge in
their beady black eyes.
Me – murderer.
And they come at me all at once and I'm falling and falling
in a mist of fur and teeth and I'm crying out, 'Squirrels eat
nuts! Squirrels eat nuts!'

MARI. That's a guilt dream, if ever I heard one.

DAVE. Do you think?

MARI. Or somewhere, deep in your psychology, you feel
castrated.

DAVE. Aye – that'll be it.

MARI. I like our little chats, Dave.

DAVE. I miss my kids.

MARI. Do you, love?

DAVE. It's better for them, you see, to live with their mother all the time. Have that continuity.

MARI. Better for them, but not for you.

DAVE. They can't stop with me anyway. My place is a bit small, grotty, and I've only got the one bedroom.

MARI. So you just see them Saturday.

DAVE. And Sunday, sometimes. I have to fit round. They've always got things on.

MARI. I suppose it's better than nothing.

DAVE. I don't take them to school, or read them a bedtime story. Sometimes they talk in their sleep – little dream voices in the dark – but I don't hear them. What they going to think of me, eh? When they're grown and they look back on their childhood?

MARI. They know you're their father. They know how much you love them.

DAVE. You reckon?

MARI. I do. And when they're grown up, they'll probably think more of you than their mother, because she'll be the one who's always had to nag them to get up, eat all their dinner, tidy their bedrooms. They'll be sick of her.
I think that's why mothers in fairy tales are always dead.

DAVE. It makes me low sometimes, Mari. I feel like nothing.

MARI. You're a wonderful dad. Those girls are very lucky.
Your wife is very lucky, if she only knew.
Think of that little mother, up in the loft. She's got something to complain about. She's gone to all that trouble – building the nest, giving birth, feeding – only to have her babies snatched from her.

DAVE. It's not like that, though. I'll get her first.
  She won't know – will she?

MARI. No.

  Sound of a key in the front door.

KATHLEEN (*off*). Hello!

MARI. What does she want?

  KATHLEEN *enters with a carrier bag.*

KATHLEEN. Dave. I thought that must be your van.

DAVE. Still chasing the lady.

KATHLEEN. Is she playing hard to get?

DAVE. Oh yes, she's a dark one.
  She's getting the nuts without springing the trap.
  Can't work out how she's doing it.

KATHLEEN. You'll catch her.

MARI. What have you got there, Kathleen?

KATHLEEN. Something for you.

MARI. Off you go, Dave.

  DAVE *exits upstairs.*

KATHLEEN (*taking a Thermos flask out of the bag*). It's a
  flask.

MARI. What do I want a flask for?

KATHLEEN. You can take it to bed. So you don't have to get
  up in the night to make yourself a hot drink.

MARI. As far as I can tell, I haven't lost the use of my legs yet.
  Not a bad idea, I suppose.

KATHLEEN. It's supposed to stay hot for hours.

MARI. Where'd you get it?

KATHLEEN. On the market. Hardware. I got chatting.

MARI. Market traders now, is it?

KATHLEEN. Take it or leave it.

MARI. How much was it?

KATHLEEN. Nothing.

MARI. He gave you it for nothing, did he?

KATHLEEN. No.
Not much.

MARI. How much?

KATHLEEN. I can't remember. I bought some other things at
the same time.

MARI. A tenner, then.

KATHLEEN. No. It wasn't –

MARI. If you can't remember –

KATHLEEN. I'll ask him.

MARI. What?

KATHLEEN. I'll ask him.
He's taking me out for a drink tomorrow night.

Beat.

MARI. While you were on the market, did you pick up my bird
food?

KATHLEEN (*fishing a bag of bird food from the carrier bag*).
This is why you've got squirrels. It encourages them.

MARI. I like to watch the birds from the kitchen window,
bustling back and forth. Especially the robins. Cheeky things.
    'A robin redbreast in a cage
    Puts all Heaven in a rage.'
When I'm washing the pots it gives me a lift. Makes me feel
like I'm getting out.
They say the robin got its red feathers as it was taking water
into Hell for the burning sinners.

KATHLEEN (*removing her coat*). Is there anything you want
doing while I'm here?

MARI. It's your half-day, isn't it?

KATHLEEN. Yes.

MARI. Good.
   I've got Bridie and Sadie coming over in a bit.

KATHLEEN. What for?

MARI. Do you want a sandwich?
   I'm still trying to get rid of that poloni.

KATHLEEN. Didn't you like it?

MARI. What do you think?
   Why couldn't you just get boiled ham? I like boiled ham.

KATHLEEN. I get bored of buying the same old thing.

MARI. You get bored too easily.
   I'm not bored.
   I'm savouring.
   I don't need any new experiences.

   MARI *exits to the kitchen.* DAVE *comes downstairs with a covered squirrel cage.*

DAVE. Got her.

KATHLEEN. It's a shame.

DAVE. You can't be sentimental.

KATHLEEN. I mean, for my mother.
   Once you've done the job you won't be coming any more.

DAVE. Oh, I expect I'll pop in to see her.

KATHLEEN. Really?

DAVE. I wouldn't begrudge your mam ten minutes' company
   now and again. She's poorly, and lonely.

KATHLEEN. She is.

DAVE (*sotto*). If I didn't know better, I'd swear she's been
   letting the squirrel out of the trap each night. Though how
   the hell she's been managing the ladder…

KATHLEEN. I expect the ladder does as it's told.

DAVE. Funny though.

KATHLEEN. Yes.

DAVE. I know she couldn't really.

KATHLEEN. No.
My mother doesn't let things go.

DAVE. Anyway, I won't stop coming.

KATHLEEN. Won't you?

DAVE. I like talking to her.
And she's the only person I know still has Garibaldis.

MARI *appears in the kitchen doorway.*

MARI. You got her, then?

DAVE. Yep.

MARI. I didn't hear her.
Her turn.

KATHLEEN. What happens next?

DAVE. I get the gun and go back up to shoot the babies.

KATHLEEN. It's quite brutal, really, isn't it?

DAVE. It's necessary.
Doesn't mean it's easy.

MARI. Have a drink before you start on the cull.

DAVE. No thanks, Mari. I'd sooner get on.

MARI. Righto.
I'll just get those picnic chairs from the shed.
We'll need them for Sadie and Bridie.

MARI *exits to the back door, through the kitchen.*

DAVE. Your cousin Sadie.

KATHLEEN. Yes.

DAVE. It's a mystery.

KATHLEEN. Yes.

DAVE. I'm sure I've seen her –

KATHLEEN. You have.

DAVE. At The Lamb and Flag.

KATHLEEN. Her mother doesn't even know she plays – never mind in a band.

DAVE. Why not?

KATHLEEN. You'd have to ask her that.

DAVE. She's good.

KATHLEEN. Yes, she is.

DAVE. Does Mari know?

KATHLEEN. No.

DAVE. How come?

KATHLEEN. We all have secrets.

DAVE. I don't.
What's yours?

MARI *enters with two folding picnic chairs.* DAVE *exits to the front door.*

MARI. Can't remember the last time we had these out. Cobwebby.

KATHLEEN. I'll stand, thanks.

MARI. Flamingoland, probably.

KATHLEEN. Why are Bridie and Sadie coming?

MARI. I've summoned them.

KATHLEEN. What for?

MARI. A rehearsal.

Pause while this registers with KATHLEEN.

KATHLEEN. Do they know that?

MARI. Do you think they'd come if they did?

MARI *sets up the chairs and dusts them down.* DAVE *re-enters.*

How's that wife of yours, Dave? Behaving herself, is she?

DAVE. Got a quote for the block paving.
Astronomical.
There's no way I can afford it. Not unless I sell a kidney or something. I wish she'd get a boyfriend.

MARI. I expect, deep down, she'll be pinning her hopes on reconciliation.

DAVE. Trouble is – if I refuse to pay for things, she gets tricky over the kids.

MARI. You have visiting rights.

DAVE. If only it were that simple.

MARI. I know it can't be easy for you, love – difficult ex-wife, two children, paying mortgage *and* rent.

DAVE. I'll be skint till I'm sixty.

MARI. Doesn't make you a very viable proposition to any other woman.

DAVE. I haven't the energy for another woman.
An ex-wife and two daughters is enough for any man.

KATHLEEN. And a stepmother.

MARI. Are your parents divorced as well, Dave?

DAVE. My mum died.

MARI. Oh dear.

DAVE. I was little. I don't remember.
My dad didn't remarry till I was older.

MARI. Was it difficult – growing up without a mother?

DAVE. Not really.
I wondered sometimes – what it was like to have a mother. The way, I suppose, other kids wonder what it's like not to have a mother.

KATHLEEN. Now, how do you know that?

MARI. Do you get on with her? Your stepmother.

DAVE. She's all right. Made my dad happy.
I wouldn't say she's like a mother to me, but she's not wicked. Not the fairest of them all, either.
When she first came to live with us, I didn't know what to do with myself. I was only fourteen and a bit of a slow developer.
One day I walked in on her, shaving her legs in the bathroom. My first real encounter with womanhood. I was terrified.
I didn't know they shaved their legs. I'd never thought of it.

MARI. Not a feminist, then.

DAVE. Who, me?
(*Realising.*) Oh, no – I don't think so.
Did you know that Queen Elizabeth the First used to shave her forehead to make her hairline higher?

MARI. That's because she never had children. My hair fell out in clumps at the front when I had mine. If she wanted to be bald, all she needed to do was have a baby.

KATHLEEN. Another good reason not to have kids.

DAVE. Have you never wanted children, then, Kathleen?

KATHLEEN. Never been married.

DAVE. You don't have to be married –

KATHLEEN. You do in this family.

DAVE. My wife's friend went to a sperm bank.

MARI. Disgusting.

DAVE. Minimal requirement, that's what men are these days. Sperm donor.
My wife's the same – she got her kids and now she doesn't want anything to do with me. She's just fine without me.

MARI. No. You can't just have babies with no fathers.
It's not right. In God's eyes, and it's not right for the babies neither.

Even if she doesn't want you.
You have to make sacrifices for your children; to make sure
they have what they need.
Sacrifice.
You can't just walk into a shop and take what you want.
You have to pay.

DAVE. It's not even as if she's got another feller. She's just not
bothered.

MARI. I suppose she can pick another bloke any time she's in
the mood.
It's not fashionable to pass judgement, though, is it?
In my day you had to behave. You had to be seen to behave.
You went to mass; confession; said your catechism.
Nowadays they do what they like.
(*Re:* KATHLEEN.) Look at her. Look at the weight on her.
That's another thing.
Me – I've always been careful what I eat.
I'd love to have a cream cake every day, but I don't.
I was taught that gluttony was a sin.
That self-restraint was a virtue.
Now they eat what they like, drink what they like –
Go with men.
It's gone too far. Too far.
And where's the justice?
Who's tried to do the right thing all her life?
Who's dying?
Sacrifice.
Paying.
Still paying.

MARI *is trembling.*

KATHLEEN. All right, Mam.

KATHLEEN *signals to* DAVE, *who gets the message.*

DAVE. I think I should be getting on, Mari.

MARI. What?
Go on. You've a job to do.

DAVE *exits through the front door.*

Glass of water, Kathleen.

KATHLEEN *exits to the kitchen.* MARI *pulls herself together.*

KATHLEEN *re-enters with a glass of murky water.*

KATHLEEN. Look at that, the water's all brown.

MARI. It goes like that. You have to run it through.

KATHLEEN. I'll have to boil it.

MARI. I didn't mean that – about you, being fat.

KATHLEEN. It doesn't matter.

MARI. You look bonny.

KATHLEEN. Dave didn't mean…
He doesn't know about Dad leaving.

MARI. We managed.

DAVE *returns with a gun and a sack.*

DAVE. Shouldn't be too long, Mari.

DAVE *exits upstairs.*

KATHLEEN. I'll tell him.

MARI. No.

KATHLEEN. Then he'd understand.

MARI. Let him wonder.
It's our life.
Keep the big things to yourself, Kathleen.
They'll always run deeper, mean more.
Take them out into the light and they look smaller.
And you see how insignificant the greatest parts of your life really are.

KATHLEEN. I don't understand.

MARI. Just another way of saying, it's none of his business.

A shot sounds from the loft: it's a dull noise, not a ringing report.

BRIDIE (*off*). Helloo! It's us.
  (*Entering*.) I've let myself in.
  Sadie's just parking. It's chock-a-block out there.
  Is that Dave's van?
  What's happened to your furniture?

MARI. St Jude's. They've had the sofa and some bits from
  upstairs so far. They're coming back tomorrow for the sideboard.

BRIDIE. Mari. It's ridiculous. You can't live here without a
  stick.

MARI. I'll have everything I need.

BRIDIE. Those old picnic chairs, though. You could have held
  on to the sofa.

MARI. Visitors don't stop long enough to justify a comfortable
  seat.

BRIDIE. That's a bit unfair.
  Though we do have to cut it short today. Sadie's just taken a
  long lunch on her flexi. She has to get back to work by half
  past two.

MARI. It won't take long.

BRIDIE. Wouldn't mind a drink, though, I'm parched.

MARI. Water's off.

  KATHLEEN *holds up the glass*.

BRIDIE (*disappointed*). Oh.
  I was looking forward to a cuppa. I can't get into my own
  kitchen today. They've started.

KATHLEEN. It'll probably be all right if I boil it.

BRIDIE. Don't bother. I'll live.
  I hate having builders in. You feel like it's not your house.
  I don't like using the toilet, or anything.

  A shot. Enter SADIE.

MARI. Sadie, love.

SADIE. Hello, Auntie Mari. How are you?

MARI. Oh, you know. Fading fast.

SADIE. Where's the furniture?

BRIDIE. St Jude took it.

SADIE. Who?

BRIDIE. What about these old picnic chairs. Do you remember them, Sadie?

SADIE. Flamingoland.

MARI. I've got the folding table as well.

BRIDIE. I don't understand you, Mari. You get rid of that lovely old sideboard and keep a crappy old picnic table.

MARI. Sorry, Bridie, did you want that lovely old sideboard?

BRIDIE. Well, no.
I don't have anywhere to put it.
It wouldn't match anything.
I have walnut.

A shot.

What the hell is that noise?

KATHLEEN. It's Dave. In the loft.

SADIE. Who's Dave?

BRIDIE. You know – who did our rat.

SADIE. Oh, Dave.
How is he?

BRIDIE. Lovely.

SADIE. Is he back with his wife?

MARI. Any day now.

BRIDIE. He asked after you last week.
Reckoned he'd seen you down The Lamb and Flag.
I told him that wasn't your sort of place.

SADIE. I go in The Pig and Whistle.

BRIDIE. That'll be it.
  Easy mistake.
  Both farm animals.

A shot.

SADIE. What's he doing?

MARI. Shooting.

KATHLEEN. Squirrels.

A shot.

MARI. So, how you keeping, Sadie?
  I'm sorry I can't offer you a coffee. Water's off. I've some
  juice in the fridge.

SADIE. Thanks.

  MARI *exits to the kitchen.*

BRIDIE (*calling after her*). I won't, thanks, Mari. I can't take
  juice, it affects my rhythm. And I wouldn't want to get
  caught short – with having the builders in.

SADIE (*looking around*). What's she doing?

BRIDIE. Lost the plot.

KATHLEEN. She's gone through everything. Forensic!
  Doesn't want anyone grubbing through her stuff when she's
  gone.
  Least of all me, for some reason.

SADIE. What's in the boxes?

BRIDIE. God knows. Can't be much, though, can it? She's
  hardly led a life of high adventure.

SADIE. And you have, I suppose.

BRIDIE. I like to think I've had some kind of horizon.
  Mari's never even been abroad.

SADIE. Marbella twice a year doesn't exactly –

BRIDIE. What are you having a go at me for?
  Since when did you stick up for your Auntie Mari?

SADIE. I'm not sticking up for her. There's just no need –

BRIDIE. Perhaps you think there's something terribly exotic coming to you. Well, let's have a look, shall we?

BRIDIE *moves towards the boxes.*

SADIE. Stop it, Mum.

MARI (*returning with juice for* SADIE). What was that about abroad, Bridie?

BRIDIE. I was just saying how you'd never been abroad.

A shot.

MARI. I'm not lucky enough to have a daughter who takes me on weekend trips to Barcelona.

SADIE. What?

BRIDIE. Oh now, Mari, you've spoiled it.
(*To* SADIE.) I've booked us a trip to Spain next weekend.

KATHLEEN. I thought you said it was Sadie's idea.

BRIDIE. You misunderstood me, Kathy. It was my surprise.

SADIE. I can't go.

MARI. Are you working weekends now, Sadie?

SADIE. No.

BRIDIE. It's only Friday night to Sunday night.

SADIE. I've got plans.

MARI. What a shame.
(*To* BRIDIE.) Will you cancel, or go on your own?

SADIE. Why don't you take Auntie Mari?

BRIDIE. Eh?

MARI. That's a lovely thought, Sadie, but I'm not well enough to travel now.

KATHLEEN. You haven't a passport.

MARI. You don't need a passport for where I'm going.

DAVE *enters, carrying the gun.*

DAVE. Unbelievable.

MARI. You got 'em.

DAVE. Not all of them.

KATHLEEN. How many?

DAVE. There's at least six.

MARI. How many you got?

DAVE. Three.

KATHLEEN. There were more shots than that.

DAVE. They move.
    Quite nippy actually.
    Bit further on than usual.
    It took us so long to get the mother.

MARI. Will you have to trap them?

DAVE. No. Shouldn't need to. This is still the best way. I just
    need to get some more shot from the van.
    Hello, Sadie.

SADIE. Dave.

    DAVE *exits to the front door.*

MARI. Now, as you're up against the clock, we'd better get
    down to business.
    We need to have a rehearsal.

BRIDIE. A what?

MARI. A rehearsal.
    I'm going to just lie back here, like I'm dead.
    Of course, on the day I'll be in my coffin – light the candle,
    Kathleen, that'll help the mood – and I want you all to just
    pretend it's my funeral and you say what you're going to say
    on the day.

    KATHLEEN *lights the candle and picks up the funeral book.*

BRIDIE. You said you'd give us time to think about it, Mari.

MARI. You've had a week.
I dare say you've scarcely thought of anything else in that time.
Kathleen.

KATHLEEN. It's a simple order of service.
Hymn.
Prayers.
Speeches.
Hymn.
Committal.
Hymn.

MARI. I've gone for deep-purple trim on the stationery.
I think it's classier than black.

KATHLEEN. Bridie speaks first, then Sadie, then me.

BRIDIE. Oughtn't you to speak first, Kathy?

MARI. That's the order I want.

KATHLEEN. So – if we take the hymn and prayers as read –

MARI. Off you go, Bridie.

BRIDIE. I'm not prepared for this yet, Mari.
I'll need to write something down.

MARI. Improvise.

BRIDIE. It's not that easy –

MARI. Oh, for God's sake, Bridie, we can't shut you up most of the time.
It's very simple. Imagine I'm dead and say what comes into your mind.

Beat.

BRIDIE (*with effort*). You're my baby sister, Mari.

MARI. Was. I *was* your sister.

DAVE *enters with the gun. Sensing an awkward moment, he passes through the room with exaggerated discretion and goes upstairs.* MARI *is now pretending to be dead.*

BRIDIE. You were my sister, Mari.
    How do you say goodbye to your baby sister?
    I remember when you were born.
    In our house. I heard you cry out in the night.
    I was seven. Then I saw you in the morning – little ratty face,
    tufty black hair, like one of those trolls you win at the fair.
    I know we haven't always been close.
    When we were children you drew all over my dolls.
    Inky Biro freckles and spectacles on Sally. Blue fingernails
    on Betty.
    (*Forced laugh.*) I couldn't stand the way you spoiled things.
    But you've done a lot for me over the years, Mari.

A shot.

That's all.

MARI *remains motionless.*

KATHLEEN. Now Sadie.

Beat.

A shot.

Just say anything, Sadie. A memory…

SADIE. When I was a kid, I used to come round for ham tea on
    a Saturday afternoon. The ice-cream van always came up the
    street about four o'clock with its Popeye jingle, and Kathy
    and me were allowed a Screwball – the one with the bubbly
    in the bottom – but we had to put it in the ice compartment
    until after our tea.

Beat.

KATHLEEN (*reading from the funeral book*). 'The longest
    lives are very short.

A shot.

As I was growing up and you were all I'd got, I used to
    worry you'd go away, or die – the way kids have fears.
    You told me that you would never leave me and that even
    though you would one day die, that day was further away
    than I could dream of, and that you would be a very old lady

by then. When a day seems an eternity, old age is unimaginable to a child.
But now – here we are.
And it doesn't seem that long.
And you're not an old lady.'

KATHLEEN *lifts her head from the page – perhaps she is improvising now...*

I don't suppose you meant to be untruthful.
Sometimes there's not much difference between a lie and a wish.
I wish.
I wish.

KATHLEEN *is overcome with emotion and unable to continue.*

BRIDIE. Oh. Oh. Mari – can we stop?

MARI *remains motionless.*

Mari. Can't you see she's upset? Why are you putting us through this?
Mari. Mari? Mari!
Oh my God. Mari!

MARI. What?

BRIDIE. Shit. Shit, Mari.

MARI. Oh, very nice.

A shot, then another.

BRIDIE. I thought you –

MARI. 'You've done a lot for me over the years – '
Doesn't quite cover it, does it, Bridie?

BRIDIE. What do you want me to say?

MARI. Here's me hoping for a few simple words of affection.
A ham tea and Popeye the Sailor –
Not exactly edifying, is it?
My obituary –
'She put a Screwball in the freezer compartment.'

BRIDIE. You expect too much.

MARI (*suddenly angry*). I expect nothing.
  And it's just as well.

  DAVE *comes downstairs with the gun and sack, which is
  now heavy with dead baby squirrels.*

DAVE. Got 'em.
  Seven.
  No trouble in the end. Just sat up and took it.

MARI (*seeing the sack*). Get out. All of you.
  Leave my house.

BRIDIE. Mari –

MARI. Look at that.
  Look at it.
  All those dead babies.
  There was never anything like enough life in this house.
  Half-lives – separation.
  And now there's nothing but death.

  DAVE *makes a hasty retreat out of the front door.*

BRIDIE. Oh, come on, Mari.
  I keep telling you, you're not dead yet.
  It's you who's bringing death up all the time: organising your
  funeral, clearing out your stuff.
  You're dwelling in it. Like you've given up.

MARI. I haven't given up.
  I'll never give up.
  Blow out the candle, Kathleen.
  You have to go, don't you, Sadie?

SADIE. I'm not in a hurry, Auntie Mari – if you want me to stay.

MARI. You go, love.

SADIE. Right.

MARI. Give me a kiss then.

  SADIE *kisses her.*

SADIE. You're cold.

MARI. I don't feel it.

BRIDIE. I'll fetch a blanket.
    Pay a call, while I get the chance.

    BRIDIE *exits upstairs.*

MARI. They say Death is like a thief, but he's not.
    He's more like a rapist.

SADIE. Auntie Mari, please.

MARI. A rapist.
    Intimate. Humiliating.
    And you cling desperately to the belief that you're more than
    flesh. That there's some part of you he can't reach.
    Can't violate.

SADIE. Mari.

MARI. To Death, you're just a body.

    KATHLEEN *and* SADIE *exchange looks. Neither knows
    what to say.*

    Kathleen.

KATHLEEN. Yes, Mam.

MARI. Where's that bird food you brought in with you?

KATHLEEN (*retrieving the bag*). It's just here.

MARI. Go put it out.

KATHLEEN. What, now?

MARI. Yes, now. Last lot ran out days ago. They're nesting at
    the moment. They've got eggs and chicks. They need extra.
    Go on. Fresh air'll do you good.

    KATHLEEN *exits through the kitchen with the bird food.*

    You get on too, Sadie. You need to go back to work.

SADIE. Right. I'll see you soon.

    Pause.

Mari. I know I'm not supposed to talk to you about this, but please, for your own sake, try not to let things that happened so long ago…
Try to let it go.

MARI. What do you mean?

SADIE. I think you know what I mean.

MARI. Why can't we talk about it?

SADIE. It's over. It's past.

MARI. You're not past. You're still here.

SADIE. I'm sorry.

MARI. What's to be sorry about?
Sadie, I know I'm not your mum –

SADIE. Oh, Mari –

MARI. Well, it's not up to me, is it? I'm not in control –

SADIE. But you are. You can be.
A victim once doesn't make you a victim for ever.

MARI. Victim?

SADIE. This talk of death being like – like a rape.
It isn't, Mari.
You're ill. What's happening to you now isn't a crime, or an assault. It's a disease. Something that happens.
I know you'll think that's easy for me to say, but it isn't. It isn't.
I know what happened. How it happened.
Mum told me. Don't blame her. I asked too many questions. What he did to you, whoever he was – I don't care who he was – it's all over long ago. I am grateful for my life, even though I know it's been so difficult for you. I will not let myself be defined by that one thing – and neither should you. I'm sorry. I've never known how you must feel when you see me. What goes through your mind.
We weren't supposed to have this conversation, I know – but maybe we needed to.

I'll visit you if you want, or you never need to see me again – I understand.

BRIDIE *comes downstairs with a blanket and stops, sensing the change in mood.*

MARI *rises from her seat and moves towards* BRIDIE. *We feel that she might strike her, but* MARI *controls her feelings with effort and simply takes the blanket.*

MARI. Off you go, Sadie.

SADIE. Mari –

MARI. Off you go.

SADIE. Right.

SADIE *exits via the front door.* MARI *moves to sit back down.*

MARI. You too, Bridie.

BRIDIE. Are you sure? I can stop a –

MARI. Out.
Get out!

BRIDIE. What?

MARI. Never come here again.

BRIDIE. What am I supposed to have done now?

MARI. Nothing – now.
But what *did* you do, Bridie?
Long ago?
What did you say?

BRIDIE. Riddles, Mari.

MARI. Now I know, Bridie.
All these years.
Suddenly.
I know.

KATHLEEN *re-enters from the kitchen.*

Beat.

BRIDIE *exits via the front door.*

KATHLEEN. What's going on?

MARI. Have the birds come?

KATHLEEN. Mam?

MARI. I'll just have a little look through the kitchen window.

MARI wraps the blanket around her and shuffles out to the kitchen. For the first time we see her frailty and the burdens that overwhelm her.

Banjo music plays.

End of Act Two.

ACT THREE

The following day – early evening.

The same.

The sideboard has now gone and all that remains is the arm-chair, the television and one of the picnic chairs.

KATHLEEN *sits in the armchair and* SADIE *on the picnic chair – waiting.*

KATHLEEN. She'll be down in a minute.

> *Beat.*

> I made her go up for a nap.
> When I got in from work she was just where I left her last night.
> Worn out.

SADIE. Maybe it's not a good time.

KATHLEEN. She knows you're here now.

SADIE. But if she's tired –

KATHLEEN. She won't be a minute.

SADIE. Mother was crying down the phone to me all night.

KATHLEEN. Does she know you're here?

> SADIE *shakes her head.*

> It's not your fault.
> Mari was all wound up anyway.

SADIE. Poor Dave. He couldn't get out quick enough.

KATHLEEN. Don't suppose we'll see him again.

SADIE. No?

KATHLEEN. Though he did say he'd visit.
Took a shine to Mari – can't think why.
He's just a nice bloke, I suppose.
But, I mean – well, the squirrels have gone now, so, you
know…

Beat.

SADIE *gives her a look.*

…He's not interested.

SADIE. You don't know that.
He's nice.

KATHLEEN. Would you go out with him?

SADIE. I might.
I like his ears.

KATHLEEN. His what?

SADIE. He has fleshy lobes – haven't you noticed?

KATHLEEN. No.

SADIE. Sign of a passionate nature.
And he has daughters, doesn't he?
Virile men produce daughters.
Oh yes. They think they're so manly when they sire sons, but
the really butch ones get girls every time.

KATHLEEN. How's that, then?

SADIE. It's something to do with how often you do it.
Honeymoon babies are always girls.

KATHLEEN. Where'd you learn that? Off a cereal packet?

SADIE. Why don't you ask him out?

KATHLEEN *scoffs.*

Why not?

KATHLEEN. Because he'd say no.
Anyway, if I went out with a divorced man it'd bring my
mother out in hives or something.

SADIE. What's she got to do with it?
 Why do you have to tell her?

KATHLEEN. I wouldn't need to.
 She's telepathic.

SADIE. She poorly.
 She's stopped work, never goes out; hardly has any visitors.
 You could do a leaping streak up Ironmarket on Christmas
 Eve and she wouldn't get to hear about it.

KATHLEEN. I'm no good at secrets.
 I haven't got your poker face.
 Mari knows I'm on my own.
 She senses it – the desperation.
 If I ever got a boyfriend, she'd smell it.

SADIE. There's nothing wrong with being on your own.

KATHLEEN. You like it.

SADIE. I prefer it.

KATHLEEN. Feller on the market asked me out yesterday.
 He was sixty if he was a day.

SADIE. Well – why not? There's nothing wrong with an older
 man.

KATHLEEN. Oh no, Sade. No.
 I haven't had sex for nearly five years. When – if I finally do
 break my duck, I'm going to need a younger man.
 Energy. Stamina.
 Enthusiasm!

They laugh.

SADIE. Five years.

KATHLEEN. Matthew.

SADIE. Oh yeah.
 Urgh.
 Forgotten about him.

KATHLEEN. Nothing to remember.
 And before that – Luke – fast on the heels of Mark.

SADIE. Are you kidding?

KATHLEEN. Nope.

SADIE. Matthew, Mark and Luke?

KATHLEEN. Gospel.

SADIE *laughs*.

And some time before the evangelists – José.

SADIE. I remember him.

KATHLEEN. I was very selfish.
Serves me right.

SADIE. I didn't mind.

KATHLEEN. Beautiful place.

SADIE. I would never have gone on my own, though – working in a Spanish bar for three months. I had to get away from my mother. It was good of you to come with me.

KATHLEEN. And then tap off and leave you on your own –

SADIE. I needed the space –

KATHLEEN. I was supposed to help you. You'd just lost your dad.

SADIE. You did help. I came back in better shape than you.

KATHLEEN. I was all right at first. Thought I'd met the love of my life, didn't I?
I was old enough to know better.

SADIE. What's to know? He was gorgeous.
Beautiful teeth.

KATHLEEN. José.

SADIE. I've never had my heart broken. Not like that.

KATHLEEN. It's crap.
I wouldn't have minded if he'd taken just a little bit longer to get over me. Two weeks it took him to stop ringing. Two weeks!
I still think of him, you know.

SADIE. Do you?

KATHLEEN. I'm like Mari – can't let things go.

SADIE. You're letting Dave slip through your fingers.

KATHLEEN. Dave won't be after me. He'd have to work too
  hard.
  He's very curious about you, though.
  Your enigmatic secret.

SADIE. Has he said anything to Bridie?

KATHLEEN. Nearly.
  Hard to believe she still doesn't know.

SADIE. Maybe she does.
  Maybe she's faking.

KATHLEEN. Waiting for you to tell her.

SADIE. It wasn't deliberate. At first I was just avoiding the
  ridicule. Then, the longer it went on, the more difficult it was
  to tell her.
  Now, if I'm honest, I like it this way.
  Little victories.
  I do love my mum, but she's the sort of person – well, you
  can't help feeling you need to keep score.

  Beat.

KATHLEEN. What happened yesterday?

SADIE. You'll have to ask Mari.

KATHLEEN. Do you think I haven't tried?
  It affects me.
  All my life. Mari – she's like a voodoo doll. Everything that
  happens to her happens to me. I can't see the pins that are
  sticking in her, but somehow I feel the pain.

SADIE. I don't suppose many people bother to ask how you are.

KATHLEEN. Occasionally somebody does, but they never
  hang around for the answer.

  SADIE *is listening.*

She won't let me stop – insists I go home. So I just lie awake
with the phone in my hand. I haven't had a drink for the best
part of a month now. (Not that I'm telling her that – wouldn't
give her satisfaction.)
What if she needs me in the night and I'm too pissed?
That's another reason I can't sleep. The doctor's given me
pills, only I daren't take them in case they knock me out and
I don't hear the phone.
You'd think there'd be an upside. I might have lost a bit of
weight with cutting out the booze, but I'm more than making
up for it in midnight snacks. I'm actually getting fatter.
Depending on how long she lasts – you'll be able to measure
the length of her life by the size of my arse.

SADIE. You're very good.
    I don't know if I could do the same for Bridie.

KATHLEEN. That's different, though, isn't it? Bridie'd have
    you back in the house like a shot. You have to fight to keep
    your distance. Me – I can get so close and no further. It's like
    she couldn't bear it somehow. And now, with all this organ-
    ising and getting rid. She's always been a control freak, but
    it's like there's something she doesn't want me to find out.

    Beat.

SADIE. She's a long time. Do you think she's all right?

    KATHLEEN *rises and goes to the foot of the stairs.*

KATHLEEN (*calling*). Mam! Are you all right?

MARI (*from upstairs, her voice tired and edgy*). Can't get the
    damn wig on straight.

KATHLEEN. Do you want me to help?

MARI (*off*). No.

SADIE (*rising*). Ooh, my back's sore.

KATHLEEN. It's those chairs.
    What is the point of picnic chairs?
    I mean, you go on a picnic so it's different to eating at home.
    So you can enjoy the outdoors, sit in the grass.

But no, Mari and Bridie have chairs.
In the middle of a field, they set the table.

SADIE. And on the beach. I remember dragging the damn
things up Mablethorpe Prom.

KATHLEEN. Right to the end, where the little train went
round.

SADIE. I've walked miles carrying those chairs –

KATHLEEN. Pick up thy cross, pilgrim.

SADIE. – but I don't think I've actually sat in one till now.

Doorbell. KATHLEEN *moves to answer, but before she can
get there…*

BRIDIE (*off*). Helloo! Hello!
(*Entering, puffing and panting.*) I did ring the bell. Didn't
like to just let myself in. Sadie! What you doing here?

SADIE. I came to try and make up –

BRIDIE. Oh – you needn't have worried.

She makes a big show of sitting in the vacant armchair.

I had to run for my bus. It's ever so warm today, I'm lath-
ered. Is the water still brown, Kathleen?

KATHLEEN. No, it's fine.

BRIDIE. I'll have a glass, then, with a drop of cordial if you've
got it. I'll not risk juice – the plumber's coming in the
morning. Did I tell you I was having a corner sink?

KATHLEEN *exits to the kitchen.*

MARI (*calling from upstairs*). Is that Bridie?

BRIDIE (*calling*). I came as soon as you rang, Mari.

SADIE. Thanks for telling me.

BRIDIE. I had to dash. Anyway, I didn't know you'd got it into
your head to come here, did I? It was just a misunder-
standing. I knew our Mari wouldn't hold a grudge.

SADIE. You kept me up half the night. Weeping and wailing. You've rung me four times today at work. You were inconsolable.

KATHLEEN *re-enters from the kitchen with a glass of lime cordial.*

KATHLEEN. Here you are, Bridie.

BRIDIE. Ta. (*Taking a swig.*) Ooh, lovely. I'm parched.
Still, it's been good to have all the windows and doors open at home. They've made that much dust. When you see it, layering up on the walnut, it makes you wonder what sort of state your lungs are in.
I've gone for stainless steel this time. I'd never have a white sink again – had to bleach it every other day just to keep it clean. Cost me a fortune in Parazone.

MARI *comes downstairs. She wears loose clothing – not nightwear – and a woolly hat. She looks exhausted, but there is an air of danger about her.*

KATHLEEN. You all right, Mam?

MARI. Hello, Sadie.

BRIDIE. Sadie – why don't you get off home? I'm sure you could do with a shower or something. Me and Mari have things to talk about. You don't need to put yourself through it.

SADIE. I'll stop a bit, thanks. I'll make a drink.

SADIE *exits to the kitchen.*

Long beat.

KATHLEEN. Do I have to make myself scarce?

MARI. No.
You make yourself comfortable.

KATHLEEN *sits, with some difficulty, in the picnic chair.*

BRIDIE. Oh, Mari. You look dog-tired.

MARI *walks slowly towards* BRIDIE.

I'm glad you've calmed down...

MARI. Who says I've calmed down?

BRIDIE (*rising*). You sit here, come on. I don't mind having the picnic chair.

MARI. I don't want to sit down –

BRIDIE. What you doing with your hat on in the house –

MARI. – about time I stood up.

BRIDIE. – are you cold?

MARI. I have something to say to you, Bridget.

BRIDIE. Well, why don't we get you cosy and comfortable first. How about a warm drink?
(*Calling*.) Sadie, is that kettle on?

MARI. I don't –

BRIDIE. Tea, Mari?

MARI. No.

BRIDIE. Coffee.

MARI. No.

BRIDIE. But you're cold. I suppose it's with you not getting any exercise. Me, I'm sweltered – had to run for my bus. I legged it here when you called, Mari. Need to sort out this little mis-understanding. I know that, I'm not avoiding it. But why don't we get you comfortable, let these two girls get back home and then you and me can have a nice quiet chat, eh? What about a milky drink –

MARI. Bridie –

BRIDIE. – with a tot of rum, or something? Do you want a blanket?

MARI. I'm not cold.

BRIDIE. Well, why have you [got a hat on]…? Oh, sorry. I forgot. What am I like, eh? Still, you could do with a nicer hat than that, if you're going to wear one. I'll pick you one up next time I'm in Harvey's. Oh, I know, why don't we ask Dave for those squirrel skins? They'd make a lovely hat,

wouldn't they? With a tail down the back – like Davey
Crockett –

With sudden energy, MARI *slaps* BRIDIE *hard across the
face.* BRIDIE *screams with pain and shock.*

MARI. You told her I was raped.

BRIDIE *reels.* SADIE *comes to the kitchen doorway.*

Deny it.
(*To* SADIE.) Is that what she told you?

SADIE. Yes.

MARI. Raped.

SADIE. Yes.

MARI. Raped.

BRIDIE. Stop it, Mari.

MARI. And I expect she also told you that you must never ask
me about it.

SADIE. Something like that.

MARI. How convenient, Bridie.

BRIDIE. What was I supposed to tell her?

MARI. How dare you?

BRIDIE. Surely you didn't want her to think that you'd been
willing.

MARI. I loved her father.
I loved him.

Long, long pause.

I never lied to you, Kathleen.
I should have told you.
As soon as you were old enough to understand –
But how could I when I'd never [talked to Sadie]… Words
turning to stones in my mouth.
Don't judge me. Not till you've heard all of it.

BRIDIE. Oh, well –

MARI. Shut up, Bridie.

> (*Re:* BRIDIE.) You. My mother and you and the nuns, lied to me about men – about suffering, blood on the sheets.
>
> (*To* SADIE.) I can see him sometimes. Same little hollow there when you smile.
>
> I wanted him and I know it was wrong, and, by God, I paid for it, but when I was with him – it's surprising –
> I didn't feel guilty.

SADIE. Who was he?

BRIDIE. Oh, for Christ's sake.

MARI. He was fair and freckled.

> Rolled his cigarettes, then ran the tip of his tongue along the paper.
>
> Pale, sensitive hands.
>
> Played in a band that came for the carnival.
>
> I'd have been about fourteen the first time I ever saw him. Then I looked forward each year, building him up in my mind. Romantic fantasies – just a teenage girl.
>
> I got to know him and by the time I was seventeen he was looking out for me.
>
> I did go with him. More than once, as it happens.
>
> I remember it. Every detail.
>
> I thought of him less as the years went on, but more again lately. When you're facing death, you need to tell yourself that you've lived.
>
> I found out I was pregnant. He'd moved on again.
>
> Still, I didn't have to worry because Bridie had been four years wed by then and no sign of a baby. Mother was a quick thinker. She sent us away to a convent somewhere down south, and when we came back, Bridie had a beautiful daughter – and I had to be married off as soon as possible.
>
> It's what happened in those days. I was young. I had nothing. No choice. No control. It was better than having you adopted out – at least I'd get to see you grow up. I had to let Bridie have you, or we'd have been out on the street.

SADIE. My birth certificate doesn't have his name –

MARI. They wouldn't let me.

BRIDIE. You wouldn't tell us.

MARI. And they never let me see him again.
He didn't know about you. He was barely more than a lad himself.
I'll tell you his name.

SADIE. No.
Not yet.

MARI. I had to promise I'd never speak of it to you – and I never would have. I always hoped. If I'd known what she'd told you –

BRIDIE. Oh, that's right, blame me. I only did all the right things. Married that hopeless stick Brian, went down the aisle a virgin, and stuck by him all those years, though he was good for nothing but shuffling round the house like an old shoe.

MARI. You didn't have to –

BRIDIE. You think you're so special. You were a groupie, Mari – and that makes you either a fool or a trollop. You think you're the first woman in history to have got knocked up by a Gypsy? Sadie's probably got siblings at every music festival in England.
I saved your face.
I raised Sadie.
She's my daughter.
Not yours.

MARI. I broke my heart watching you grow up.
Never being able to kiss your knees, or call you mine.
When Kathleen was born, it made things easier – and harder… and… Oh, I've got it all wrong. All my feelings – they're like fog. I can't find my way through.

MARI *sits in the armchair, exhausted.*

BRIDIE. I knew this would happen. I dreaded it. I knew you wouldn't be able to just go quietly and leave everything – you're a spoiler, Mari.
You're messy.
How do you think I felt all these years, knowing you could take her from me any time you wanted?

You – so fertile. Fat pink babies popping out of you like
plums. If Jack hadn't had enough of you and buggered off,
I've no doubt you'd have had a whole tribe.
Why can't I just have Sadie? You've got Kathleen.
(*To* SADIE.) I was protecting Mari. I didn't want you to
think she –
Well, as far as I knew, it was rape, practically. She wasn't
much more than a child and he was older – more a man of
the world. How was I to know she'd thrown her legs in the
air? That's the first I've heard of any ecstasy.

SADIE. Are you all right, Kathy?

KATHLEEN *nods.* BRIDIE *rummages in her handbag, finds
cigarettes and lighter, and exits via the front door. Long
pause.*

I'm sorry.

Pause.

KATHLEEN. When did you find out?

SADIE. I needed a passport for Spanish exchange.
Must have been fifteen or sixteen.

KATHLEEN. And Bridie told you...

SADIE. Not in so many words – sort of implied it. But she
sugared over everything with how much her and Dad loved
me. God, she's a monster. Letting me think –

KATHLEEN. Why didn't you tell me?
We were friends.

SADIE. It wasn't up to me.
I didn't think it was.
Poor Mari.

KATHLEEN. Did you never want to ask her?

SADIE. I don't know. Maybe.
You know me. Not saying things gets to be a habit.
And I had my dad, didn't I? I had him to think of. He loved
me and he brought me up.

KATHLEEN. You did better than me.

SADIE and KATHLEEN *look at* MARI, *who has closed her eyes.*

She must have hated my dad.

SADIE. He just wasn't what she wanted.
You've been in love.
She was trapped, wasn't she?

KATHLEEN. Oh, that's very easy for you to say.
The love child.
Free spirit.
I was born in the cage.
With her, pecking at me.
Never knowing why.
Never understanding.
What am I supposed to do now, eh? Roll my eyes in my head
– say –
'Ah, now I get it!'
'That explains a lot!'
It doesn't.
It doesn't.

SADIE. But what else can we do?
Just soak it up. Keep going. Adapt.
Life's like a maze. You truck along until you come to something that blocks the path. So, you take a turn – right or
left.

KATHLEEN. Mari didn't take a turn, did she – all those years
ago. She just stayed where she was and stared at the wall.

They both look at MARI, *who has apparently fallen asleep in
the chair.*

Why don't you get off?
I'll stay with her till she wakes up.

SADIE. Are you sure?

KATHLEEN *nods.* BRIDIE *enters.*

BRIDIE. You going, Sadie?

SADIE *walks past her without acknowledgement and exits via the front door.*

Sadie.

KATHLEEN. Bye, Bridie.

Beat.

BRIDIE. I'll call.

BRIDIE *exits via the front door.*

Beat.

MARI. Kathleen.

KATHLEEN (*unsurprised*). Yes?

MARI (*opening her eyes*). When I'm in my coffin, in the chapel of rest, I don't want anyone to visit me.
Nobody.
I don't want anyone to look at me when I'm dead.

KATHLEEN. All right.

MARI. You don't have to write it in the book.
I know you'll remember.

Slow banjo music plays.

End of Act Three.

ACT FOUR

Some weeks later.

The same.

A bare stage, except for the three boxes, now centre and dressed with a tablecloth. This 'table' is set with tea, sandwiches, pork pie and Fondant Fancies on paper plates, covered in cling film. Crisps in a paper bowl.

BRIDIE *is standing, drinking tea and eating crisps.* SADIE *comes downstairs.*

BRIDIE. How is she?

SADIE. She'll be all right.

BRIDIE. I didn't even notice, until she got up to speak.

SADIE. How could you not notice?

BRIDIE. I've never seen her like that.
　　Total personality change.
　　Have you ever seen her like that?

SADIE. Not for a long time.

BRIDIE. What a showing-up.
　　Such language.
　　I thought the priest was very understanding.

SADIE. I expect they can just glue the top back on the lectern.

BRIDIE. I cleaned the hall up as best I could.
　　Couldn't find a bucket.

SADIE. There wasn't much.

BRIDIE. She can't have had anything to eat.

SADIE. I'll make her a coffee.

　　SADIE *crosses to the kitchen.*

BRIDIE (*indicating food*). She won't want any of this, will she?

SADIE. I doubt it.

BRIDIE. Do you want any?

SADIE. Lost my appetite.

> SADIE *exits to the kitchen.* BRIDIE *peels off the cling film and helps herself to pork pie.* SADIE *reappears from the kitchen.*

> Kettle's on.

BRIDIE (*peeking under the tablecloth*). So – now we get to find out what's in these.
I needed to see her, Sadie.

SADIE. She was definite.
Nobody. Not even you.
Especially not you.

BRIDIE. What did it matter?
She wouldn't know.

SADIE. It was her body.

BRIDIE. But she said – funerals are for the living.
I'm alive. I've got to carry on.
I wanted to say goodbye.

SADIE. You wanted to be sure.

BRIDIE. You'd no right denying me.
She was my sister long before she was your mother.

SADIE. Oh, get over it, Mum.
It wasn't up to us.
She didn't want anyone looking at her.
Kathy and me were only following her wishes.
I never saw her either.

> SADIE *exits to the kitchen.*

BRIDIE (*calling*). Is today a special amnesty, or are you officially speaking to me again?

> *Beat.*

For God's sake, Sadie, it's been weeks.
Don't be so childish.
You've got to give me the chance to explain.
Why is everyone so sorry for Mari?
What about me? I'm the one with nothing.

SADIE (*reappearing with a coffee jar*). How can you say that?
Mari never had much and lost almost everything she ever had –
First her lover, then me, then her husband, and now her life.
She never even owned her own home.

BRIDIE. And a three-bedroomed semi with a Magnet kitchen is the be all and end all?
I'm a widow.
I only ever had you to console me and I lost you long ago.

SADIE. You didn't lose me – I moved out.

BRIDIE. Why?

SADIE retreats into the kitchen again to make coffee.
BRIDIE follows, staying onstage and leaning on the kitchen doorway.

You're not married. You don't even have a 'partner', or whatever it is they call it these days. I'm on my own – you're on your own.
I thought, when your dad died...
Kathy was never away from here.
She loved her mother.
You don't love me.
Look how much she did for her.
Can you honestly say that you'd do the same for me?
Can you?

Beat.

That's right. My daughter is only borrowed.
Borrowed.
You were always hers. Before you knew it, you were hers. I saw the way she looked at you. You didn't understand, but you must have felt it.

SADIE (*appearing briefly*). I was a kid. I didn't feel anything.
All I cared about was where the next packet of sweets was
coming from.

BRIDIE. She played the martyr, she did.
Suffering stigmatic – when, really, she had everything.
Even had unbridled lust.
That was the last straw, that was. All I ever got was the occa-
sional clammy grope from Brian. And let me tell you, 'inex-
pert' does not cover it. God knows, I tried to get rid of him,
but he would put up with it –
Great chalky stick.
Thirty-eight years, Sadie.
Mari managed to drive Jack away after about eighteen months.
He loved her, you know. He wanted her in the beginning.
Even converted for her – and you have to swallow more than
the body of Christ to do that. He came from a good family
too. In fact, I think his father was a Buffalo.
They could have been happy.
They went to a caravan at Humberston Fitties for their hon-
eymoon, and they must have got on all right because she was
pregnant with Kathleen when they came back.
Mari was determined to be miserable.
Punished Jack every day of their married life – poor sod.

SADIE *comes through, past* BRIDIE, *with a mug of coffee.*

SADIE. Stop it, Mum.

BRIDIE. You don't know, Sadie. You don't remember. You've
got this sickly notion about a dying woman, crying for her lost
love and her stolen child, and I know it's earwax. Mari fabri-
cated this romance up over the years – rewrote it in her head.
We tell some whopping lies in our lives, but we always save
the biggest ones for ourselves.

SADIE. You let me think my father was a sex offender.

BRIDIE. How often do I have to say it, Sadie? As far as I
knew –

SADIE. All my life you behaved as if music was a kind of
social disease.

BRIDIE. It's not my fault you can't sing.

SADIE. You didn't want to give Mari the satisfaction –

BRIDIE. Your father played in a two-bit skiffle band, Sadie – that doesn't make you Maria Callas.

SADIE. You knew who he was, didn't you?

BRIDIE. No.

SADIE. Well, you can't hide him from me any more. I know his name.
Mari told me.

BRIDIE. What? Are you going to go looking for him?
Oh, well, I'm sure he'll be delighted to see you.
What do you think you'll find? A pot-smoking pensioner with a bald head and a ponytail down the back.

SADIE. Did he have a ponytail?

BRIDIE. I don't know, I never saw him.

SADIE. You're lying.

BRIDIE. I was Mari's sister, not her Siamese twin. I was a married woman, with a home of my own. I didn't know where she was or who she was with. I should have thought that was obvious.
Sadie, tell me you're not going looking for him.
You'll be disappointed.
If he's not a geriatric beatnik, he'll have gone the other way – had a wash, got married and settled down. Is that how you want to find your Gypsy dad? Your wandering minstrel? Pricking out his marigolds while the grandkids run round his legs?

SADIE. Maybe I've found him already.
Maybe I knew where he was all along.

KATHLEEN *comes downstairs, looking rough. She has been drunk, sick and is now sobering up. She has a slight cut over one eyebrow.*

BRIDIE. Kathy, love. How are you feeling now?

KATHLEEN (*weakly*). Better, thanks.
Sorry.

SADIE. I made you a coffee.

BRIDIE. Sit yourself down, Kathy. Though, I must tell you, if you need to throw up again, I couldn't find a bucket.

KATHLEEN. I'll be all right now.

> KATHLEEN *takes the coffee and sits on the bottom step.*
> BRIDIE *takes a cigarette from her bag and lights up.*
> KATHLEEN *and* SADIE *look at her.*

BRIDIE. What?
It can't matter now.
The council don't care.
It's not her house any more.
There's puke in the hall!

> *They stare her down.* BRIDIE *gives up and exits via the front door.*

KATHLEEN (*groaning*). Bad, wasn't it?

SADIE. Epic.

KATHLEEN. What did I say?

SADIE. You don't remember?

KATHLEEN. Bits.

SADIE. You were doing quite well, until you leaned forward on the lectern.

KATHLEEN. Right.

SADIE. We thought you'd knocked yourself out, but you sort of bounced.
Then Father Donal came to your assistance.

KATHLEEN. Tosser.

SADIE. That's when it turned nasty.

KATHLEEN. I just wanted to finish my speech. He wouldn't let me finish.

SADIE. I've not seen you like that for years.

KATHLEEN. I'd learned to take it.

SADIE. We got you outside and walked you round a bit.

KATHLEEN. I remember.
I was sick in the Garden of Remembrance.

SADIE. Then we got you into the car and you passed out.
I waited with you and let you sleep it off a bit while Bridie
went back and saw the last of the service. We couldn't hang
about, there was another funeral waiting.

KATHLEEN. So she sang 'O Mother Most Pure' on her own?

SADIE. We'll never know.

KATHLEEN. Then what?

SADIE. We got you back here, you were sick again in the hall.

KATHLEEN. Oh, yes.

SADIE. I got you upstairs, where you threw the rest down the
loo and fell asleep on the bathroom floor. I put a towel under
your head and sat with you until I was sure you weren't
going to choke or anything.

KATHLEEN. Thanks.

SADIE. How you feeling now?

KATHLEEN. Still a bit, you know, but okay.
Oh God, Sadie. All Mari's planning.

SADIE. I think she knew something like this would happen.
That's why she insisted on just the three of us being there.
Sort of damage limitation.

KATHLEEN. That make me feel great, that does.
My mother arranges her own funeral around the expectation
that I'll be off my face.

SADIE. At least you didn't give that little performance in front
of all her church friends, or Dave.
You called the priest some things I've never heard of.

KATHLEEN. I haven't had a drink for months.

    I tried, Sadie. I really did.

    Even on the day she died, I didn't.

    Each day since I've been battling, battling to stay off it.

    This morning I told myself I'd just have a little one, to steady myself.

    If I'd had anything else to do, it would have been easier.

    Normally you'd have organising, arrangements.

    It's the way people get through the first few days, isn't it?

    But she left me with nothing to do.

    It was sorted.

    All I had to do was buy the Fondant Fancies.

    I nearly lost it in the supermarket.

    Stupid.

    I was going up and down the aisles and I couldn't find the cakes.

    I don't know why – they were where they always are.

    I started to panic.

    Couldn't breathe. Couldn't see.

    Pictures flashing in my head.

SADIE. Pictures.

KATHLEEN. A bird on a bonfire.

    Bright-eyed. Burning.

    And this terrible flapping.

    Poor thing.

    I don't know why I keep seeing it, but it won't go away.

    Or the smell of scorched feathers.

SADIE. We all loved her.

    Even Bridie.

KATHLEEN. I saw her – just after, at the hospice, still in the bed.

    But not again.

SADIE. I wish I'd told her about the band.

KATHLEEN. Why didn't you?

SADIE. Because Bridie doesn't know.

    It didn't seem right for Mari to know something she didn't.

    She is my mum.

KATHLEEN. Will you tell her now?

SADIE. I might.

KATHLEEN. I wish I was like you.
    You have a secret.
    Mari said some things mean more if they're hidden.
    She was right.
    A secret is a beautiful thing.
    Something living.
    Sustaining.
    I reckon she lived her whole life from that brief passion.
    Fed it.
    Fed on it.

SADIE. How did she look?

KATHLEEN. Peaceful.

SADIE. I saw her the day before.

KATHLEEN. The nurse told me.

SADIE. I bumped into Dave on my way out.

KATHLEEN. I think he was the last person she saw before she
    slipped down...

    KATHLEEN *almost breaks down, but somehow masters her
    emotions.*

    When I got there that night, she wasn't conscious any more.

SADIE. He kept coming, like he said.

KATHLEEN. He's good.

    Pause.

SADIE. I'm thinking of going travelling.

KATHLEEN. Are you?

SADIE. I've been wondering for a while. I'm not happy at work.
    I've been saving up.
    I was thinking I'd need a flat-sitter.

KATHLEEN. Oh yes?

SADIE. I just remember Dave saying he was in a little bedsit
and I wondered if he'd look after the flat for me. No rent,
just bills. Might suit him.

KATHLEEN. It might.

SADIE. But will you be seeing him? Now Mari's gone.

KATHLEEN. I don't know.

SADIE. Give him a ring.

KATHLEEN. Why don't you ring him?

SADIE. I just thought – well, you know him better than me.

KATHLEEN. Do I?

SADIE. If it bothers you, just let me have his number.

KATHLEEN. I have it somewhere.

SADIE. No rush.

KATHLEEN. How soon are you thinking of going?

SADIE. End of next month.

KATHLEEN. No rush?
    What about Bridie?

SADIE. Bridie'll be here when I get back.
    What are you going to do with yourself?

KATHLEEN. No idea.
    No idea.

SADIE. Shall I clear these things?

KATHLEEN. Don't you want any?

SADIE. Not really.

> SADIE *clears the cups.* KATHLEEN *exits to the kitchen,*
> *returns with a bin bag and chucks all the food away.*

Shall I wash up?

KATHLEEN. No. You go.

SADIE. Are you sure?

KATHLEEN. I'll be going home myself now.
Get cleaned up.

SADIE. You're all right?

KATHLEEN. I'm fine.

SADIE. Do you want a lift?

KATHLEEN. I'll walk.
Fresh air'll do me good.

SADIE. I'll go, then.

KATHLEEN. Don't forget this.

KATHLEEN *separates the three boxes and gives one to*
SADIE.

SADIE. Thanks.

SADIE *exits.* KATHLEEN *quietly folds the tablecloth.*
BRIDIE *enters.*

BRIDIE. You're okay now, Kathy?
I'm off. Our Sadie's giving me a lift.
Can't lug that box on the bus, can I?
Give it here, then.

KATHLEEN *hands over the box.* BRIDIE *gives it a shake.*

Don't suppose there's any avoiding that bloody vase.
If I treat it rough enough I might have broken it by the time I
get home.

KATHLEEN. Oh, Bridie, before you go, I meant to ask you –
Do you want Mam's bird table?

BRIDIE. Her what?

KATHLEEN. Her bird table. It's the only thing she didn't
think of.
I don't have a garden and neither does Sadie.

BRIDIE. Oh.
What's it made of?

KATHLEEN. I don't know. Pine.

BRIDIE. I have walnut.

KATHLEEN. It's for outside.

BRIDIE. No, love. Thanks all the same.
I don't really like birds.
All bones and feathers. Give me the creeps.
Besides – putting food out tempts the undesirables, doesn't it?
And Dave's a lovely lad, and all that, but I don't think it's
worth having squirrels chomping through my soffits.

KATHLEEN. No.
Never mind. I'll leave it here.
Maybe the next people will like it.

BRIDIE. Yes, that's right.
It'll probably be a family.
That kind of thing's nice for children, isn't it?

KATHLEEN. Bye, Bridie.

BRIDIE. You need a holiday.
They've some good offers in Sunny Climes.

KATHLEEN. I'll think about it.

BRIDIE. Try not to dwell, love.

BRIDIE *exits.* KATHLEEN *stands, alone and uncertain.*
Slowly, she kneels on the floor and opens her box. It's full of
documents, which she picks out one by one.

DAVE (*off*). Helloo!

KATHLEEN. Oh, no.

DAVE *enters cautiously through the front door.*

DAVE. Hello, Kathleen.

KATHLEEN. Dave. You missed Sadie and Bridie.

DAVE. I saw them driving off.

KATHLEEN. Oh.

DAVE. I wondered how you were.
I'm sorry about your mum.
I would have come –

KATHLEEN. It was invitation only.

DAVE. Have you cut your eye?

KATHLEEN. It's nothing.

Beat.

DAVE. So, how are you?

KATHLEEN. I'm all right.

DAVE. You look… tired.

KATHLEEN. I got pissed.

DAVE. Ah.
Understandable.

KATHLEEN. Aggressive and abusive.

DAVE. So, Mari's funeral didn't go quite as planned, then?

KATHLEEN. No.
(*Laughs.*) No, it didn't.

DAVE. I wish I'd gatecrashed now.

KATHLEEN (*warm*). I know I've said this loads of times,
Dave, but thank you. Thank you for going to see Mari. She
thought you were wonderful.

DAVE. No problem.

KATHLEEN. In fact, I think you were the last visitor she was
really aware of.

DAVE. Oh? I was there the day before –

KATHLEEN. She lost consciousness.

DAVE. I see.
It's quite nice there, isn't it – in the hospice?
I mean, for somewhere you go to – you know.
I thought it'd be depressing, but it wasn't.
I liked that big display they've got in the entrance, about St
David.

KATHLEEN. I never read it.

DAVE. They say he lived to be over a hundred, and all he ate
was bread and watercress.
Amazing.
And he used to stand up to his neck in a lake of cold water,
reciting scripture – in Wales!
I took the kids camping in Wales last year.
It was freezing. And we had Polartec.

KATHLEEN *laughs*.

I was wondering – say if you don't want to – but would you
let me buy you a drink sometime? Tonight, maybe? Well –
perhaps an orange juice tonight.

KATHLEEN. Oh.
I don't know.
I don't think so.

DAVE. I just thought it might help – today.

KATHLEEN. It's not that, you know.

DAVE. Maybe another time.

Beat.

She really cleared everything.

KATHLEEN. Everything.
I'll just take the last bits from the kitchen and hand in the
keys.
I grew up in this house.

DAVE. She was a great person, Mari.

KATHLEEN. Yes.

DAVE. But she wasn't right about everything.

KATHLEEN. Where were you thinking of going?
For a drink.

DAVE. I usually go in The Lamb and Flag, about eight-ish –
There's a band on tonight.
A good band.

KATHLEEN. Really?
She never said.

DAVE. But I thought that might be a bit noisy.
So, I was wondering – maybe The Cock and Bull?

KATHLEEN (*smiling*). Are you serious?

DAVE. I'll take you wherever you want to go, Kathleen.

KATHLEEN. It's Kathy.

DAVE. Okay then.

Beat.

What you looking at?

KATHLEEN. I just noticed your ears.

DAVE. My what?

KATHLEEN. I like music.

DAVE. You don't have to say now.

KATHLEEN. About eight-ish?

DAVE. I'll be there.
If you fancy.

KATHLEEN. I might.

DAVE. Good.

Beat.

I'll leave you to it, then, shall I?

KATHLEEN. I'm nearly done.

DAVE. See you then.

KATHLEEN. Yes.

DAVE *exits.* KATHLEEN *turns her attention back to the box.*

Now then, Mari.
What have you left for me?

KATHLEEN *reaches into the box and pulls out the yellow vase. She laughs in surprise, laughter which quickly turns to weeping. She rocks gently back and forth, holding the vase close to her.*

A spotlight picks up on SADIE, *playing her banjo with furious energy.*

The End.

A Nick Hern Book

Flamingoland first published in Great Britain as a paperback original in 2008 by Nick Hern Books Limited, 14 Larden Road, London W3 7ST, in association with the New Vic Theatre, Newcastle-under-Lyme

Flamingoland copyright © 2008 Deborah McAndrew

Deborah McAndrew has asserted her right to be identified as the author of this work

Cover image: Jo and Katie McAndrew in Mablethorpe, 1973.
Photograph by John McAndrew
Cover design: Ned Hoste, 2H

Typeset by Nick Hern Books, London
Printed and bound in Great Britain by CPI Antony Rowe, Chippenham, Wiltshire

A CIP catalogue record for this book is available from the British Library

ISBN   978 1 84842 001 4